FELLWALKING WITH
WAINWRIGHT

FELLWALKING WITH
WAINWRIGHT

18 of the author's favourite walks in Lakeland
with photographs by

DERRY BRABBS

Michael Joseph London

CONTENTS

First published in Great Britain by Michael Joseph Limited
44 Bedford Square, London WC1
August 1984
Second Impression November 1984

Wainwright, A.
    Fellwalking with Wainwright.
    1. Walking–England–Lake District
    2. Lake District (England)–Description and travel–Guide-books
    I. Title
    796.7'22   DA670.L1

    ISBN 0 7181 2428 6

Typeset, printed and bound in Great Britain by
W.S. Cowell Limited, Ipswich

(Endpapers) View East from Pike o'Blisco
(Page 1) The Helvellyn Range from Fairfield
(Page 2-3) The North Western Fells from Hindscarth
(Page 4-5) Derwentwater from Maiden Moor
(Page 224) Sunset over Derwentwater

LOCATIONS OF THE WALKS DESCRIBED IN THIS BOOK:

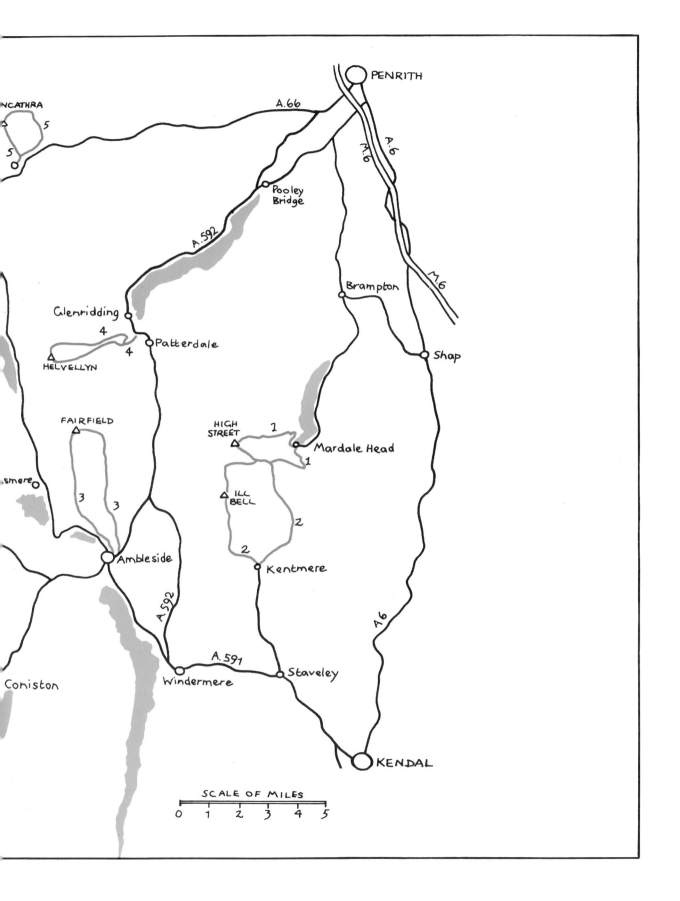

NCATHRA

5

5

A.66

PENRITH

A.6

M.6

M.6

Pooley
Bridge

A.592

Brampton

Glenridding

4

4

Patterdale

HELVELLYN

Shap

FAIRFIELD

HIGH
STREET

1

Mardale Head

1

smere

ILL
BELL

2

3

3

2

2

Ambleside

Kentmere

A.592

A.6

Coniston

A.591

Windermere

Staveley

KENDAL

SCALE OF MILES

0   1   2   3   4   5

1 HIGH STREET AND HARTER FELL

FROM MARDALE HEAD   (7 MILES)

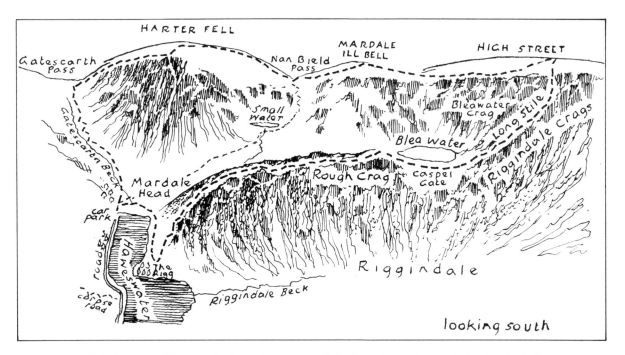

High Street, a fell named after a Roman road, is the culmination, at 2718 ft, of a lofty range rising from the valleys east of Windermere and extending for many miles at an elevation everywhere in excess of 2000 ft before finally descending to lower levels near the foot of Ullswater. This range forms a spine along the eastern fringe of Lakeland, providing a splendid full-day's march at a consistently high altitude, but is distant from the areas most favoured by fellwalkers and is comparatively unfrequented, appealing mainly to lovers of mountain solitude. Often I have been quite alone on High Street and seen no other person.

The late M. J. B. Baddeley, whose guidebook to the Lake District I revered more than the Bible in my early wanderings, described High Street as 'one of the least interesting of the Lake mountains'. One does not lightly question the judgment of so eminent an authority, but with this opinion I profoundly disagree.

High Street's few visitors are usually engaged on a traverse of the range and they find its broad summit merely a long grassy promenade with little of interest except the view westward. But if approached from Mardale Head, as described in this chapter, the ascent lacks nothing in beauty and exhilaration, the route following a rocky ridge, straight as an arrow, that leads directly to the top of the fell amidst mountain scenery of a very high order. I rate this a classic climb, a connoisseur's way to the summit.

(Opposite) Harter Fell from the old corpse road

I never go to Mardale Head now without thinking of a summer's day more than forty years ago when I walked over Gatescarth Pass and saw the valley of Mardale for the first time. It was a lovely vista. The floor of the dale was a fresh green strath shadowed by fine trees and deeply inurned between shaggy heights; beyond, receding in the distance, was Haweswater, then a natural lake. It was a peaceful scene, the seclusion of the valley being emphasised by its surround of rough mountains. Mardale was a bright jewel in a dark crown . . . I remember that day so well. Many early memories have faded, but not this one. Down in the valley, I went along the lane to the Dun Bull between walls splashed with lichens and draped with ivy. There was no welcome for me at the inn, which for centuries had been a meeting place of farmers and shepherds and the scene of many a festive occasion. It was empty, unoccupied. Around the corner was the small church amongst fine yews: it was a ghostly shell, the interior having been dismantled and the bodies in the graveyard exhumed for reburial elsewhere. The nearby vicarage and a few cottages were deserted and abandoned. This was the hamlet of Mardale Green, delightfully situated in the lee of a wooded hill, but now under sentence of death. Birds twittered in the trees and my footsteps echoed as I walked along the lane but there was no other sound, no sign of life. Even the sheep had gone. There were wild roses in fragrant hedgerows, foxgloves and harebells and wood anemones and primroses in the fields and under the trees, all cheerfully enjoying the warmth and sunshine; but there would be no other summers for them: they were doomed . . . Manchester Corporation had taken over the valley and built a great dam. The lake would be submerged beneath a new water level a hundred feet above. Already the impounded waters were creeping up the valley. Soon the hamlet of Mardale Green would be drowned: the church, the inn, the cottages, and the flowers, would all disappear, sunk without trace, and its history and traditions be forgotten. The flood was coming and it would fill the valley. Nature's plan for Mardale was being over-ruled. Manchester had another plan, to transform Mardale into a great Haweswater Reservoir. And no doubt be very proud of their achievement . . . I climbed out of the valley to Kidsty Pike. Looking back at Mardale Green from a distance, its buildings no longer seeming forlorn but cosily encompassed by trees and its silent pastures dappled by sunlight, I thought I had never seen a more beautiful picture. Nor a sadder one.

Haweswater today

When Manchester Corporation destroyed the
sylvan beauty of Mardale by drowning it beneath
the waters of a huge reservoir, they made a slight
penance for their sins by constructing a tarmac
road alongside to the head of the dale and providing
space for cars to park at its terminus, a concession
appreciated by fellwalking motorists who can thereby be quickly transported to the heart of a scene of
mountain grandeur unsurpassed in the district.
Harter Fell's wall of crags is dominant and seen
intimately; High Street's wild recesses are more
distant to the right and partly hidden by the ridge
along which the ascent is to be made. Yes, there is
an awesome grandeur hereabouts. Once there was a
foreground of pastoral loveliness and shy charm,
too, but that has gone, lost forever.

A much-trodden path leaves the car park but soon
bifurcates at a wall corner, the left branch leading to
Gatescarth Pass and the other heading half-right for
Nan Bield, both popular walkers' routes. In fact, the
path may be said to trifurcate; a third track, the one to
be used for the ascent of High Street, goes sharp
right around the head of the reservoir and crossing
Mardale Beck. At this point, although early detours
are generally not advisable when a long day's march
lies ahead, a visit to the charming waterfall of Dodderwick Force can be made by walking upstream for
a few minutes. Returning, the path is resumed alongside the reservoir and rises to a grassy col above the
wooded promontory known as The Rigg.

Originally it was planned to build a rest-house or
small hotel here to replace the Dun Bull, served by a
new road along the west side of Haweswater, and the
site would have been ideal for walkers coming down
from the mountains, but other opinions prevailed
and in the event the road was made along the east
side and the new hotel sited midway, which is incon-
venient for walkers who have to travel a further two
miles on tarmac to reach it.

(Right) Dodderwick Force

From the col, the path doubles back at a higher level, climbing gradually, at first on grass and then amongst rocky outcrops, with a sharp zigzag to reach a wall on the crest of the ridge. Looking over the wall there is a splendid full-length view of Riggindale, now without a habitation, the former farm buildings at the mouth of this wild recess having also been casualties of the flood. From this viewpoint, the rocky escarpment of Rough Crag, above which the route continues, can be seen extending into the distance; around the head of the dale is a rim of crags, and on the far side rises the peaked summit of Kidsty Pike in profile.

Looking back over The Rigg and the reservoir to the fellside beyond, the zigzags of the old corpse road can be discerned, this being the way along which the dead of Mardale Green were carried, strapped to the backs of horses, for interment at Shap, eight hilly miles distant. This practice ceased in 1729 with the building of Mardale Church and the granting of a right of burial in a graveyard adjoining.

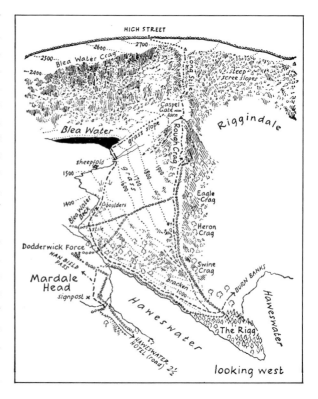

Riggindale

The path, still climbing, soon attains the top of the narrowing ridge and discloses a view to the south of the wild basin of Small Water below Nan Bield. Now at an easier gradient, it threads a way amongst outcrops, the scenery becoming more impressive as height is gained, and so reaches the summit cairn of Rough Crag where the route ahead is suddenly revealed. This is a place to halt and look around. Directly in front is the last stage of the ascent: across a grassy depression the rocky stairway of Long Stile rises steeply, leading unerringly up to the great curve of the skyline of High Street. To the left of Long Stile is the forbidding declivity of Bleawater Crag, the scene of a recent accident when a schoolboy fell to his death, and below it are the dark waters of Blea Water, better seen by a short stroll southwards. Behind is the imposing mass of Harter Fell, and to the immediate right the great gulf of Riggindale: from the edge of its cliffs an aerial view is obtained of this wild and lonely valley, now a sanctuary and grazing ground for deer and fell ponies.

I was standing here a few years ago, looking down into Riggindale, when a huge bird took off from the crags below and with two lazy flaps of its wings soared effortlessly across the valley and alighted on the topmost rocks of Kidsty Pike opposite, a flight accomplished in a few seconds only. There was no doubting its identity. It was a golden eagle . . . A decade ago, a pair of these magnificent birds made the crags around Mardale Head their home. Not for 150 years had the species been seen in Lakeland, but now they have returned, to the excited delight of ornithologists and all privileged to witness their soaring flight. To prevent disturbance, wardens of the Royal Society for the Protection of Birds kept a day and night guard within sight of the first nesting-places and the exact location was kept secret, their surveillance being relaxed as the birds became established in the district. There are many Eagle Crags in Lakeland, one of the buttresses of Rough Crag being so named, the inference being that in past centuries the district was a favourite habitat of eagles. It is a testimony to the wild seclusion of Mardale that it was chosen by the birds for their return. They are welcome. In a world fast becoming mainly concerned with material advantage, it is reassuring to have this evidence that nature conducts its affairs unchanged. The eagles are back, and it is the best thing that has happened to Mardale in the past fifty years.

High Street and Blea Water from Rough Crag

Long Stile and High Street from Rough Crag

Beyond the summit of Rough Crag, the ridge descends to a depression known as Caspel Gate. There is no gate, the name signifying a pass, but there is no pass either: a simple descent, left, on grass, leads down to Blea Water, but there is no way down into Riggindale on the right for ordinary walkers.

Ahead is Long Stile, a steep rocky spur of intimidating aspect, but there are no difficulties in its ascent and a final scree path emerges suddenly and abruptly on the plateau of High Street at a large cairn erected for the guidance of walkers descending by this route. The transition in scenery is immediate and complete: all is grass, there is not a rock in sight, and an easy five-minute perambulation brings one to a triangulation column alongside a crumbled wall.

This is the summit of High Street.

Although lacking in natural features of interest and having nothing to explore, the summit of High Street offers a splendid opportunity for rest, relaxation and quiet and undisturbed meditation: all is peaceful, and if the larks are singing overhead it is a blessed experience to be up here above the world and its worries. But only visitors of lively imagination will fully appreciate their surroundings. Any person so favoured may recline on the grass and witness, in his mind's eye, a pageant of history, for he has been preceded here by the ancient Britons who built their huts in the valleys around, by the Roman legions who marched across the top of the fell, by the Scots invaders who were repulsed on the Troutbeck slopes, and later by the dalesfolk who gathered on this lofty height for annual meetings and festivities.

Harter Fell and Blea Water from High Street

If visibility is clear there is a wonderful panorama westwards where the mountains of Lakeland are seen arrayed in a tumult of peaks on the distant horizon.

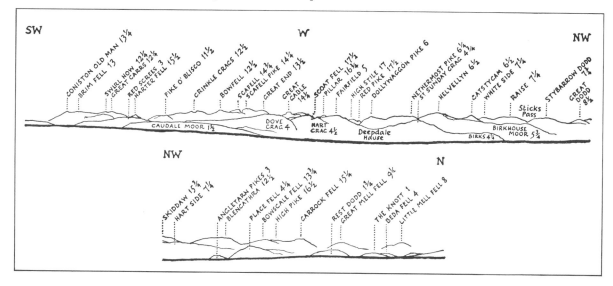

By crossing the tumbled wall on the top of High Street and strolling westwards for a couple of minutes the Roman road is reached. This remarkable highway, still distinct and used as a footpath, is, at 2700 ft, the highest Roman road in the country. It linked the fort of Galava (Ambleside) and the fort of Brovacum (Brougham): a long day's march high above the valleys, its course being very direct, almost a beeline, proving the topographical knowledge of the surveyors and the ability of the engineers to master rough terrain – and the stamina and endurance of the legions who tramped this mountainous twenty-mile marathon.

The flat top of High Street is a smooth plateau of grass, a quiet and lonely wilderness, but in days gone by it was the venue of an annual meet of dalesfolk, always a great occasion of revelry and merriment, with horse-racing and wrestling and other sporting events, barrels of beer and hampers of food being carried up to provide an ample and memorable feast.

The Roman road on High Street

The tale is told that on one such occasion a dedicated hunter of foxes, a man named Dixon, upon seeing a fox run along the top and disappear over the edge of Bleawater Crag chased after it full tilt and fell hundreds of feet over the escarpment, coming to rest on the screes far below, where he raised himself, pointed in the direction the fox had gone and shouted excitedly to the horrified onlookers on the cliff top 'It's gone o'er theer, it's gone o'er theer!', and then dropped dead from his injuries, a victim of fanatical enthusiasm.

In those days the fell was better known as Racecourse Hill and appeared as such, in large lettering, on early Ordnance Survey maps. The name has been retained and still features on recent issues but in a much smaller type.

In early Victorian times the annual meet was transferred to the Dun Bull at Mardale Green, where the festivities continued apace on a day in the third week in November until brought to an end by the closure of the inn a hundred years later.

Blea Water

The next objective is the stony summit of Mardale Ill Bell, a mile south-east, and the walk to it, descending slightly across a pathless upland prairie, is easy and pleasant but featureless. A better plan is to go straight to the rim of Bleawater Crag and by following it along enjoy striking aerial views of Blea Water a thousand feet below, backed by Rough Crag and with the heights around Mardale in the further distance. Blea Water is large and circular and the deepest tarn in the district, reputedly occupying the crater of an extinct volcano although more likely to be of glacial origin.

At the wide depression between High Street and Mardale Ill Bell, a path will be found leading to the latter summit where there are two cairns, the southern one having a good view of the upper Kentmere valley. There is nothing here to suggest the presence of a line of crags nearby to the north, a fine vantage point for an appraisal of the topography of Mardale and its surroundings.

Haweswater and Small Water from Mardale Ill Bell

From the top of Mardale Ill Bell, at 2496 ft, a distinct and stony path goes down to Nan Bield Pass. I remember this as a thin and sketchy track, but obviously it has suffered much foot-traffic in recent years. On the descent, there occurs a glorious prospect of Haweswater and Small Water, in line one above the other: a picture no walkers with cameras can resist. Then, quite suddenly, after rounding a small hillock with striated rocks, Nan Bield is reached.

In my opinion, Nan Bield is the grandest of all Lakeland passes, being a narrow and steep-sided col, the climb to its top at 2100 ft being immediately followed by a sharp descent. There is a substantial wall-shelter on the summit. The pass was a trade route in the days of packhorses and down on the shore of Small Water are three stone refuges, roofed with slabs, built for the benefit of travellers overtaken by storms or darkness: these are low and entered by crawling, to the consternation of the many resident spiders.

The path on both sides of the pass is a series of zigzags to aid progress over the steep ground, but on the Mardale side it has become a river of stones, tiresome to descend, where thousands of impatient boots have scoured away the original well-graded path.

A descent to Mardale Head may be made from Nan Bield if time is pressing or the steep slope of Harter Fell directly opposite seems too much for tired limbs: the climb, however, is less formidable than it appears, the gradient soon easing into a gentle rise to the summit of Harter Fell.

Nan Bield Pass

The topmost cairn on Harter Fell, at 2539 ft, bristles with discarded iron fenceposts, forming a weird superstructure to the stones.

Every step now is downhill to Mardale Head and the path turns in that direction only to be halted on the edge of a tremendous crag. Here is disclosed the full length of Haweswater two thousand feet below: a most impressive view and the highlight of the whole journey.

(Right) The summit of Harter Fell

(Below) Haweswater from Harter Fell

There is palpably no way down the crag other than by falling over it, and the path turns sharply away south-east to skirt the declivity until advantage can be taken of a rock-free descent to the top of Gatescarth Pass in view below.

The path coming over Gatescarth Pass from Longsleddale is a joy to descend. This was also a trade route in days gone by, and the zigzags made centuries ago to ease the passage of laden ponies and driven sheep over steep ground have survived intact, unlike those on the Mardale side of Nan Bield and, having a grassy surface, are a pleasure to walk upon. I am a great enthusiast for zigzag paths: they have been engineered with care, always following the easiest line of ascent or descent. Habitual beeliners who cannot be bothered to go left and then right and left and right and commit the sacrilege of cutting corners, have not been active here and the path remains unspoilt. It is a lovely way down to Mardale Head and has the added bonus of a stream alongside, the first running water encountered since leaving Mardale Beck and a source of refreshment for thirsty throats and aching feet.

The descent of Gatescarth Pass

On the descent, the view forward opens up to reveal High Street and Rough Crag framed between the towering cliffs of Harter Fell, where the eagles on their return to Lakeland unsuccessfully established their first eyrie and then abandoned it for other sites, and the steep rise of Branstree on the right. After the last zigzag, a leisurely saunter down a gentle grass slope leads to Mardale Head and the waiting car.

2 THE KENTMERE ROUND
FROM KENTMERE VILLAGE   (12 MILES)

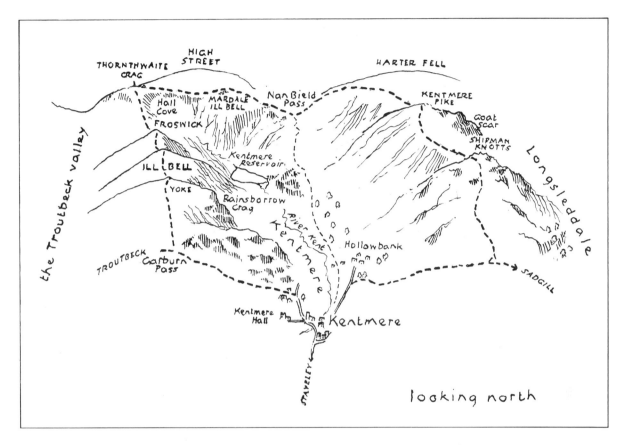

Many motorists approaching from the south regard their sighting of Windermere as the beginning of the Lake District and head eagerly along the A591 until it comes into view, unheeding or unaware of a side road signposted 'Kentmere' as they pass through the village of Staveley en route.

By doing so, they miss the loveliest of the lesser-known Lakeland valleys. Kentmere is delightful in all seasons, the lower reaches alongside the River Kent being especially charming. After three miles along its tree-lined road, in more open country, Kentmere Church is seen ahead on a small elevation. Only a few dwellings cluster round the church, but populated outposts nearby help to earn for Kentmere the status of a village although there is neither an inn nor a shop. The narrow road does not invite the parking of cars, but outside the church it widens to cater for the cars of worshippers and is taken advantage of by those who come to worship on the fells. This is the place, the only place, to leave a car.

(Opposite) The head of Kentmere

A short lane opposite the church leads to Kentmere Hall, the most interesting residence in the valley, with a ruinous 14th-century pele tower of four storeys linked by a staircase, and a vaulted cellar. The adjoining manor house, of rather later date, was originally the seat of the Gilpin family; a notable member was Bernard Gilpin, born here in 1517, who had a distinguished career in the Church and became known as 'The Apostle of the North'. The building is now occupied as a farmhouse.

Kentmere Hall

The first objective of the walk is Garburn Pass, to gain a foothold on the Ill Bell ridge, an imposing and effective barrier between the valleys of Troutbeck and Upper Kentmere. I have a long affection for this lofty ridge: it is in view from the windows of my home ten miles away, sometimes bathed in sunlight, sometimes sombre, often beheaded by low clouds and seemingly doubling its stature under a mantle of snow. It is a good barometer too, for when its outline dissolves in mist there will be rain in Kendal within an hour. Ill Bell is the dominant height on the ridge and has two satellites, Yoke and Froswick: all have very steep slopes above the Troutbeck Valley but these are bland and rock-free except where pierced by abandoned quarries. On the Kentmere side, the declivity is even steeper and breaks into precipitous crags. Travel along the crest, however, is simple and free from hazard; mist has no terrors but robs the walker of a superb view of Windermere and the western fells. A clear day is preferable for this expedition.

The walk starts from the church and goes along the road beyond until abreast of a cluster of houses and farm buildings on the left. The Garburn path passes between these and emerges into open pastures. In the first field on the left, and seen by looking over a wall, is a huge rock, apparently a craggy outcrop but in fact a tremendous boulder that has fallen from the heights above; it is one of the largest in the district. It is known as Badger Rock, or Brock Stone, and is a well-known local landmark although having little fame outside the valley. There are rock climbs of varying difficulty on its steep face.

(Right) Badger Rock
(Below) The new Kent Mere

A little further along the path there is a downward view of Kentmere Hall amongst trees and, beyond it, a mile down the valley, is the unexpected sight of Kentmere's new lake. Until 1840 there had always been a shallow natural lake on the flat strath south of the church. It was known as Kent Mere and gave its name to the valley, but in that year it was drained to provide more land for cultivation: a purpose not entirely achieved, much of the reclaimed ground remaining too marshy for the plough and even for grazing. Analysis of the former bed of the lake in the present century revealed the presence of diatomaceous earth which, when extracted and processed, proved a valuable insulation material and led to the establishment of a works near the site. The draining of the lake was probably a factor in the erratic flow of the Kent thereafter, causing the promotion of an Act of Parliament authorising the construction of a reservoir at Kentmere Head to ensure regular supplies of water to the many woollen and corn mills down the river. In recent years, the supply of the diatomaceous earth became exhausted and the works closed; following the cessation of operations, a new lake, narrow but half a mile in length, came into being. This is now privately owned and intended as a nature reserve.

The path, everywhere pleasant, steepens as the top of Garburn Pass is approached below a line of crags up on the right, through which an adventurous scrambler may force a passage to gain the ridge above more directly – a deviation not worth the extra effort.

I once saw an adder basking in the sunshine on a large flat stone at the side of the path hereabouts, one of only two I have ever seen in the district, the other being near Tarn Hows. There was no ill feeling; indeed the beautiful creature winked at me as I passed. The day was peaceful, the sun warm, the stone comfortable. All was well with the world and life was good; besides, the prey didn't seem too wholesome, so why bother to attack? The adder resumed its siesta and I went on my way.

Garburn Pass is thought to be a section of an old road that cut across the south-eastern fringe of Lakeland, the path being of cart width, and this theory is supported by its naming as Garburn Road on the Troutbeck side, where it is a lane between walls, and by its obvious continuation as a broad track, crossing the low fells from Kentmere to Longsleddale, whence presumably it traversed Mosedale and descended Wet Sleddale to Shap.

The summit of Yoke looking towards Ill Bell

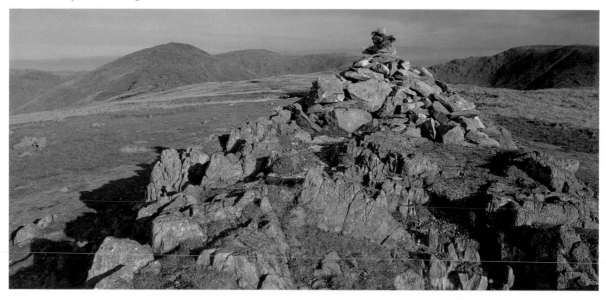

When the top of Garburn Pass is reached, a splendid prospect of the western fells unfolds suddenly and to good effect after the limited confines of the climb to it. Here the walk parts company with the path which continues down to Troutbeck, and turns sharp right along a rising moorland, marshy in places, and narrowing as height is gained. The first summit reached is Yoke, with a cairn at 2309 ft but little else of immediate interest: the ground eastwards, however, soon breaks into the tremendous Rainsborrow Crag, which falls precipitously into the depths of upper Kentmere, a refuge for foxes and a resort of rock-climbers, and the most imposing natural feature in the valley. The presence of this fearful crag is not suspected from the summit of Yoke, and attention is mainly focussed on the graceful cone of Ill Bell further along the ridge.

The summit of Ill Bell, 2476 ft, can be bypassed from Yoke along a level track across the western flank, but is of unusual interest and commands such fine views that it should certainly be visited. A multiplicity of cairns, three of long-standing, augmented by others that have sprouted in recent years, crowd the small top and suggest that the summit has some great significance in mountaineering history or is the apex of a major rock climb, but in fact has no such distinctions. Nevertheless, it is a splendid airy perch, and with the ground falling away out of sight all round, gives the impression of an island in the sky. It is a rough and stony top, with cairn-building material in profuse supply. Its special joy is a superb full-length view of Windermere.

From the northern edge, there is a graphic picture of the continuation of the route, looking over the next summit on the ridge, Froswick, to its culmination beyond at Thornthwaite Crag. It will be seen that the walk lies along the crest of a profound drop into the head of Kentmere far below, the effects of erosion and landslips being much in evidence, the eastern slope of Froswick in particular being a chaos of tumbled rocks and scree.

The summit of Ill Bell

A rough descent from the top of Ill Bell is followed by a gentle rise to the summit of Froswick, 2359 ft, which from some directions appears as a minor replica of Ill Bell. Froswick was the first mountain I saw at close quarters: I was toiling up Scots Rake out of upper Troutbeck, head down and watching where I was putting my feet, when I halted to look up and saw the peaked summit of Froswick overtopping the slope, much higher than I expected and seeming almost unattainable. The sight was quite awesome, even frightening: I had little appreciation of scale and perspective in those days. Upon ultimately gaining the ridge and looking back along it, Froswick was seen as an insignificant height dwarfed by Ill Bell behind it.

The obelisk on Thornthwaite Crag

From Froswick's small and neat summit there is a simple descent to a small depression on the ridge and a long rise to Thornthwaite Crag, the path being joined in the later stages of the climb by the Roman road coming up Scots Rake.

Thornthwaite Crag is easily identifiable from afar by its tall obelisk, a conspicuous landmark. This is a pillar of stones 14 ft high and commanding a view of four valleys, beautifully constructed and a fine monument to the skill of its unknown builder.

(Opposite) Thornthwaite Crag and Froswick from Ill Bell; (below) Looking back to Rainsborrow Crag

From the top of Thornthwaite Crag, 2569 ft, the walk changes direction, turning east and abandoning the Roman road which heads for High Street, now in full view, and following the edge of an escarpment with the wild amphitheatre of Hall Cove far below. Marshy patches along here are the source of the River Kent, developing into trickles that combine to form a well-defined stream, seen far below as it winds down the valley to Kentmere Reservoir. This considerable sheet of water will have been glimpsed from the Ill Bell ridge, but is here seen in full dimension.

In the mid-19th century, no fewer than fifteen mills on the banks of the Kent were drawing water from the river for driving their machinery, this being their only source of power, and often in times of drought production was halted or restricted. To avert this occasional failure of supplies, an Act of Parliament authorised the construction of reservoirs in the valleys of the Kent and its tributaries, the Sprint and the Mint, to be administered by commissioners (the mill owners) for the purpose of impounding water that could be released when needed to maintain an adequate flow in the rivers. Five reservoirs were proposed but only one was made: Kentmere Head Reservoir, as it was then named, completed in 1848. The others were never proceeded with because the cost proved greatly in excess of the estimate, and an alternative source of power – coal – became readily available as means of transport improved. The industrial use of the reservoir has ceased but, surprisingly, it has never been adapted to serve domestic needs.

The head of Kentmere from below Ill Bell

Kentmere from above Hall Cove

The walk continues eastwards to the top of Mardale Ill Bell, 2496 ft, the prefix being added to the name to distinguish it from the better known and more imposing fell of Ill Bell visited earlier in the walk. From the rugged outcrops south of the summit, there is a splendid retrospect of the whole ridge traversed from Garburn Pass, Rainsborrow Crag now being seen in profile and the steep and scarred declivities of Ill Bell and especially Froswick well displayed.

From Mardale Ill Bell, the route coincides for a time with that of Walk 1, a distinct path going down to Nan Bield Pass and affording views of Small Water and Haweswater. The good track crossing the pass, an old trade route, offers a quicker return to Kentmere if desired and is a delightful descent, at first down unspoilt zigzags and then across open moorland, reaching the valley by the side of a rocky bluff known as Tongue Scar, a long-established haunt of badgers, and proceeding thence to the village in charming surroundings. But for those determined to do the walk as planned, the steep-facing slope of Harter Fell must be tackled. The summit may be bypassed when easier ground is reached by heading south, contouring the fell until a ridge path is joined and the summit of Kentmere Pike reached.

The top of Kentmere Pike is uninteresting, the only feature being a triangulation column alongside a wall that continues without a break along a declining ridge to the Kentmere – Sadgill 'road' two miles south and is a perfect guide in misty conditions. Although the top of Kentmere Pike is merely a grassy sward, the ground eastwards soon drops away into the wild hollow of Settle Earth, an uncompromising downfall of crags and boulders and scree.

Alongside the wall, the path descends easily on grass. It was about here one Sunday midday that I came across a local shepherd and his dogs taking a rest. He seemed to want to talk and told me that he had spent the morning chasing foxes out of the Longsleddale crags and over into Mardale, his reason for this extraordinary behaviour being that he had heard of a fox-shoot planned to take place that afternoon around the head of Longsleddale. He was a supporter of fox-hunting with hounds which ensured a swift death for the foxes, but totally opposed to the shooting of them, this practice too often resulting only in wounding them, sometimes so badly that they could no longer search for food and died miserably from hunger and their injuries. A very ordinary man but with a concern for the welfare of wild creatures that raised him above most other men. 'They'll shoot nowt today!' he said with a satisfied smile.

(Above) Settle Earth from Goat Scar   *(Opposite) The valley of Longsleddale from Goat Scar*

Further down the ridge, Goat Scar juts out above Longsleddale and the short detour to its cairn is strongly recommended, this being a magnificent viewpoint. Longsleddale is seen aerially from the wild head of the valley to the lovely wooded lower reaches while, looking back, the grim fastnesses of Settle Earth can now be appreciated.

Now the ridge levels and there is a slight rise to the last summit of the day, Shipman Knotts, 1926 ft. This is a rocky upthrust of the ridge, with outcrops everywhere and very steep slopes falling to the woods of Sadgill. From its cairn, Goat Scar is seen in profile and across the deep trench of Longsleddale the cliffs of Buckbarrow Crag buttress the easy upper slopes of Tarn Crag where another obelisk stands on the skyline, this being a survey post built by Manchester Corporation when constructing a tunnel to convey their Haweswater aqueduct; when its purpose was served, it was left to rot and is already partially collapsed.

(Above) Tarn Crag from Shipman Knotts *(Opposite) Kent Falls*

Leaving Shipman Knotts, it is necessary to continue down on the west side of the wall to avoid being trapped by an unclimbable wall lower down. The descent is without incident: there is little vestige of a path but by keeping in the company of the wall, the cart-track coming up from Kentmere and going over to Sadgill is reached near its highest point. About here, a little-used path branches off and descends directly to Green Quarter on the outskirts of Kentmere village, but it is much better to go along the cart-track and enjoy, when some small barns are reached, a classic view of the head of Kentmere around which the course of the day's march can be traced. Then a lane is entered, this joining the tarmac road to Hollowbank.

The last stage of the walk is down this road to the left, with a possible short detour when a signposted lane comes in on the right: by going a few paces along this and trespassing down a small field, Kent Falls may be seen in a charming setting.

It is well not to anticipate a drink or a meal in the village. For such deserved refreshment, after retrieving the parked car up the steep incline to the church, it will probably be necessary to travel down the valley to Staveley or Kendal. It should be in the nature of a celebration for the accomplishment of a memorable walk.

3 THE FAIRFIELD HORSESHOE
FROM AMBLESIDE   (11 MILES)

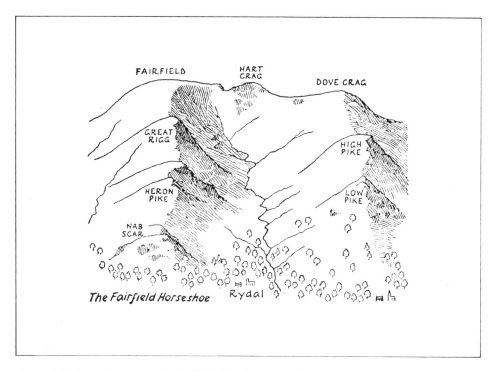

One of the best-known walks in Lakeland is around the great arc formed by Fairfield and its two southern ridges enclosing the deep valley of Rydal Beck. Four summits in excess of 2500 ft and four of lower altitude are visited during the course of the walk, the whole round being at a high level and providing a succession of contrasting views – grim mountain fastnesses seen intimately, and lovely lakes and valleys seen distantly. In recent years, this has become a very popular expedition and the full circuit is now the objective of an annual fell race. The whole course is known as the Fairfield Horseshoe and is sufficiently well defined to make any errors of route finding unlikely.

Fellrunners will complete the whole round in less than two hours without seeing anything other than the track before them. I admire those who can perform such feats. I envy their fitness but not their achievements; racers and record breakers seem to me to be out of place on the high fells. Mountains are there to be enjoyed, and enjoyed leisurely. I never could travel at speed on foot, nor have I ever wanted to. Sour grapes don't enter into it. My preference always is to walk slowly, halting often to look around and see what is to be seen.

Fairfield is too good to be treated merely as a checkpoint. The Horseshoe deserves a full day and is liberal in its rewards for those who linger and look.

(Opposite) The Fairfield Horseshoe from Todd Crag

The walk may be started along either of the two southern ridges. Although my natural inclination is to do a circular walk clockwise, I prefer in this instance to travel anti-clockwise, partly to avoid the steep initial climb to Nab Scar, partly to take advantage of easier gradients in ascent, but especially to enjoy the morning approach to High Sweden Bridge, always a delightful start to a day on the fells.

A purist determined to do the ridge, the whole ridge and nothing but the ridge, will leave Ambleside by way of Low Sweden Bridge, reach the ridge wall as it emerges from the valley trees and follow it upwards without deviation.

Non-purists like myself, out for pleasure, will leave Ambleside along the steep Kirkstone road and turn off at Sweden Bridge Lane to a gate at the end of the tarmac. I was once standing here when a fox came running down the rough lane beyond, squeezed through the bars of the gate and disappeared into a private garden nearby, completely ignoring my presence. It was followed a minute later by a straggling pack of hounds. Fox-hunters say that a fox enjoys the excitement of being chased and has no sense of fear until it is actually caught. I'm afraid I don't believe a word of it. The fox I saw was terrified: it was running for its life, and knew it.

Beyond the gate, Sweden Bridge Lane is delightful, rising between walls with a glorious view of the Vale of Rydal deep in a mountain surround. Further on, the lane enters a woodland, now having Scandale Beck tumbling down a ravine alongside, heard but not seen until the charming centuries-old High Sweden Bridge is reached.

Sweden Bridge Lane

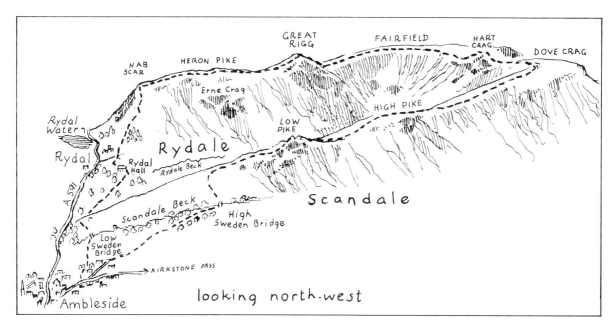

High Sweden Bridge

Scandale Beck, flowing under High Sweden Bridge, is the last running water encountered on the route until the return, some hours later, to valley level. After taking a photograph of the bridge, as every visitor does, and resisting the temptation to linger in this lovely spot, it is crossed and a grassy slope is climbed from it to the wall on the ridge between Scandale and Rydale, the latter here coming into view. This is the Horseshoe proper and from here on all walkers become purists without option. The wall is followed upwards, easily but with one awkward step to negotiate, to the rocky top of Low Pike, 1657 ft, the first summit on the ridge and scenically the best. Low Pike is the objective of the annual guides' race at Ambleside Sports. Although of modest altitude, it commands a splendid prospect of the other ridge of the Horseshoe with Fairfield dominant at the head of Rydale and of the woodlands of Rydal Park down below to the left. The lakes of Windermere, Esthwaite Water, Coniston Water and Rydal Water are all in view from this vantage point. Ahead, due north, is the next summit, High Pike.

There is a descent from Low Pike to a depression on the ridge and a steep climb follows to the top of High Pike alongside the wall, which hereabouts is worthy of notice: it is still in pristine condition despite nearly two centuries of storms and strong winds. Everywhere, even on the steepest ground, the stones are laid in persevering horizontal courses and with such skill in construction that they are securely wedged without the use of mortar. The men who built the stone walls that run for miles over the high fells of Lakeland were experts at their craft; they had to collect the stones from the ground nearby and cut them to shape on the site, they often spent the nights on the fells to save travelling and their reward was eight pence a day. They are forgotten. The walls they built so well are monuments to these unkown craftsmen. Other men have been knighted for less.

The wall

(Opposite) The summit of Low Pike

(Above) High Pike and Bakestones

The top of High Pike has nothing of interest to delay progress. It is flat and grassy, not at all the sharp peak suggested when seen from below. The summit cairn stands at 2155 ft on the edge of a decaying crag overlooking Scandale. The view westwards is obstructed by the high wall which, although still a work of art, is rather a nuisance to those who like to sit at ease and study panoramas.

Without any inducements to linger, the route is continued along the rising ridge to Dove Crag, which hitherto has been hidden by High Pike but is now revealed ahead and reached by a simple ascent in the company of the wall.

Walkers arriving at the top of Dove Crag on a first visit will be surprised to find no sign at all of any crag, the summit cairn at 2603 ft occupying a small rock platform on a broad and featureless plateau. But any disappointment is more than countered by the excellence of the panorama, the view over the gulf of Kirkstone to the far eastern fells, not yet seen during the walk, now being revealed.

Here the route turns north-west, still following the wall, which is now sadly crumbled and only a shadow of its former self, but walkers with a liking for exploration should continue due north down the slope to reach the brink of the crag that gives its name to the fell. Here one can look down Easy Gully, but the tremendous overhanging cliff can only be suspected by the great void below: a small wall marks the limit of exploration and is a warning that should be heeded, for the ground beyond breaks away in a fearful precipice. From a safe stance, however, the wild beauty of Dovedale, a tangle of knobbly hillocks and wooded slopes, can be seen far below descending to the Patterdale valley at Hartsop: a lovely picture enhanced by range after range of lofty fells in the background.

Dovedale from the top of Easy Gully

The ridge wall descends to a wide depression before the rise to the next summit, Hart Crag. In this hollow I was once joined by a wandering foxhound. It is not unusual to come across solitary hounds that have lost the scent or perhaps merely be out for exercise: they are always friendly. On another occasion a hound spent the day with me, joining me from the doorway of the Kirkstile Inn at Loweswater, climbing with me to the top of Hen Comb, patiently waiting for half an hour while I took photographs and made notes, and then returning with me to the valley where it disappeared into the inn without a word or sign of goodbye. It was nice to have company that needed no conversation.

(Top left) High Bakestones; (top right) The summit of Hart Crag; (above) Fairfield from Hart Crag

From the depression, it is possible to make a very steep and pathless way down into Rydale in emergency but the main route now climbs to the rocky top of Hart Crag, 2698 ft, which overlooks both Rydale and Dovedale's wilder and less attractive neighbouring valley of Deepdale. The summit is defended on both flanks by crags, those on the north side falling into the grim hollow of Link Cove. Fairfield is now directly ahead and reached by descending to a narrow col formerly known as The Step and encompassed by cliffs: an exciting situation. There is no hindrance to progress, however, and a steep pull up the facing slope leads to the long plateau of Fairfield.

The walk along the top of Fairfield to the summit cairn at 2863 ft is easy underfoot, on soft turf. Sensational views down into the wild upper reaches of Deepdale can be obtained by keeping close to the edge of the northern cliffs. There now no wall to act as guide in mist, and this is the one place on the route where there could be confusion in murky conditions, some of the many cairns not necessarily indicating lines of approach or descent and being dangerously misleading. In clear weather there are no problems and a fine panorama can be enjoyed.

(Right) Cofa Pike
(Opposite) Grasmere, Coniston Water and finally the sea

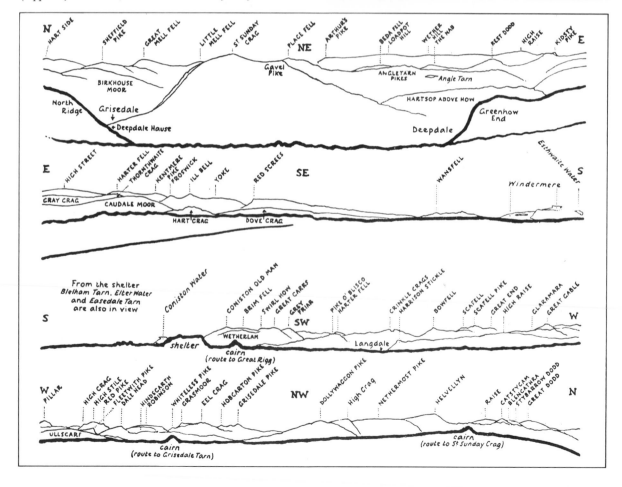

From the summit cairn of Fairfield a detour is recommended to the sharp peak of Cofa Pike, 300 yards along the ridge descending due north in the direction of St Sunday Crag. This is a neat rocky upthrust blessed with a most impressive view of the northern cliffs of Fairfield, the highlight of the expedition. Also well seen from this vantage point is the tremendous bulk of Helvellyn, towering into the sky across the deep trench of Grisedale, and the more shapely outline of St Sunday Crag rising beyond the depression of Deepdale Hause.

St Sunday Crag

Returning to the top of Fairfield, and with two-thirds of the walk now completed, the other leg of the Horseshoe has yet to be traversed, the route heading due south from the summit cairn along a narrowing ridge to the prominent dome of Great Rigg directly in front. This is the last fell of any significance; its summit, at 2513 ft, is attained by a short climb and has nothing of interest except a large cairn and a carpet of level turf that many a cricket ground would envy. The western slopes of Great Rigg are grassy, but the eastern side is a sharp declivity, rough and rocky, falling into the head of Rydale. Rydale, incidentally, is a name that does not appear on Ordnance maps but, as it contains Rydal Beck and ends at Rydal, the name is appropriate for this long valley.

(Opposite) The north face of Fairfield   *(Above) The summit of Great Rigg*

A long descent from Great Rigg leads to an undulating section of the ridge where two minor summits share the name of Heron Pike, the higher being 2003 ft. Neither deserves to be called a pike and there are no herons: the name is probably a corruption of Erne, a cliff on the Rydale flank having the name of Erne Crag. A lack of interesting features on the ridge hereabouts is compensated by the increasing beauty of the valleys ahead and now not far distant.

Next follows the last stage of the Horseshoe: an easy descent to Nab Scar, 1450 ft, directly overlooking Rydal Water, to which it falls in slopes so steep and craggy that even the most ardent purist will prefer to take the tourist path and turn away south-east. This path is steep and severely eroded, making the descent the roughest part of the whole journey. Some repairs have been effected by wardens of the National Park and steps constructed: a contentious improvement, many walkers feeling that steps are for going up to bed, not for climbing mountains. At the foot of the steepness, the path descends easier ground, passing a plantation and so reaching the lane that climbs into Rydale from the nearby A591.

Nab Scar from Rydal Water

Nab Scar is a very familiar object overlooking the A591 alongside Rydal Water and is invested with a certain romance because of its associations with the Lake Poets who lived at the base of its wooded slopes. It has a subterranean tunnel carrying the Thirlmere Aqueduct but there are no visible signs of it and nothing mars the attractiveness of this colourful height.

Scandale Beck at Low Sweden Bridge

The return to Ambleside may be made along the busy main road, but a much more pleasant alternative is available on public footpaths passing alongside Rydal Hall and through the grounds of Rydal Park to Low Sweden Bridge, where Scandale Beck comes tumbling down a wooded ravine in spectacular cascades. From a farm across the bridge, tarmac lanes lead into Ambleside.

HELVELLYN BY THE EDGES
FROM PATTERDALE   (8 MILES)

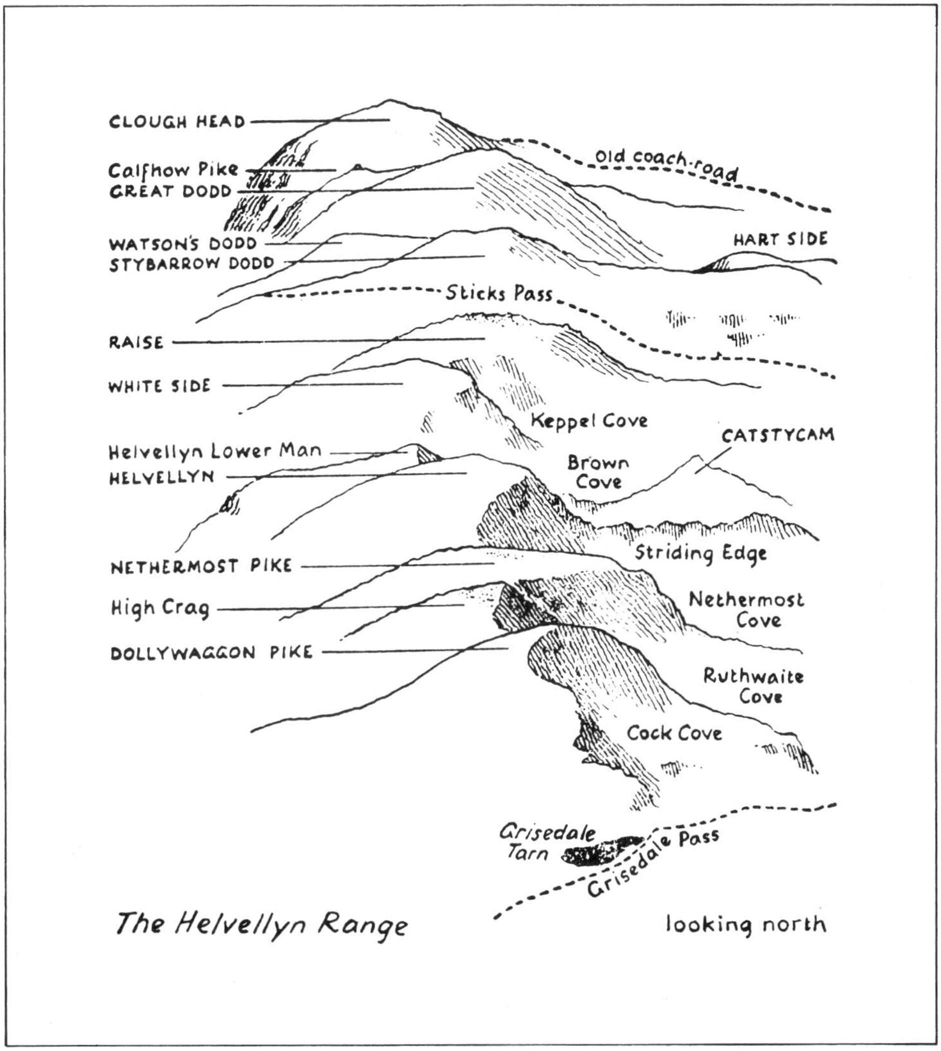

CLOUGH HEAD
Calfhow Pike
GREAT DODD
WATSON'S DODD
STYBARROW DODD
Old coach-road
HART SIDE
Sticks Pass
RAISE
WHITE SIDE
Keppel Cove
CATSTYCAM
Helvellyn Lower Man
HELVELLYN
Brown Cove
NETHERMOST PIKE
Striding Edge
High Crag
Nethermost Cove
DOLLYWAGGON PIKE
Ruthwaite Cove
Cock Cove
Grisedale Tarn
Grisedale Pass

The Helvellyn Range   looking north

Helvellyn is the pivot of a long range of fells extending from Grisedale Tarn to Thirlspot and forming a high barrier between the valleys of Thirlmere and Ullswater. It is also, at 3118 ft, the dominant height, overtopping not only its satellites but all the other fells in the district except the Scafells. The range is the most extensive continuous area of high fell country in Lakeland and its complete traverse an obvious challenge to active walkers. But the star attraction is Helvellyn itself.

(Opposite) Helvellyn from Cofa Pike

Helvellyn is climbed more often than any other mountain in Lakeland and, more than any other, it is the objective and ambition of tourists who do not normally climb. Thousands of people of all ages reach its top every year and there are very few days, if any at all, when no visitor calls at the wall-shelter on its summit. There are many reasons for its popularity: its lovely name is a magnet; legend and immortal poems are associated with it, conferring an aura of romance; the views are comprehensive and extend to far distances, making a fine panorama; the summit has a reputation as the best place to watch the sun rise; it overtops all else for miles around; no mountain is more accessible from a main road; and it has as its principal feature Striding Edge, the most exciting of all walkers' routes; and although it can be a grim place in wild weather, it is generally a very friendly giant, proud to have so much attention. There is some mystical quality about Helvellyn that inspires affection, and its devotees return often.

Helvellyn is a Jekyll and Hyde mountain. It is unfortunate that the ascent is usually made by well-trodden paths up the western slopes from the main road along its base, this flank, although benign and free from hazard, being dull and relatively uninteresting. Approached from the east, however, it presents a very different picture, the climb being exhilarating and in beautiful and impressive surroundings and the mountain revealing the other side of its character, a stern and forbidding appearance. This is the way to go for those who prefer a spice of adventure and sustained interest on their fellwalking expeditions.

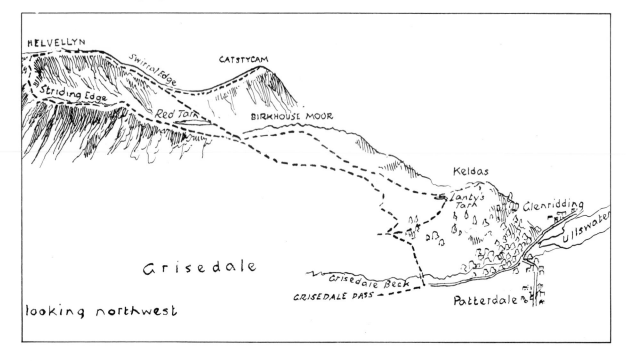

Grisedale

Just beyond Patterdale Church on the road to Glenridding, a side road branches off to the left and rises gradually into Grisedale. In a short mile, at the end of the tarmac (often cluttered with parked cars), a signposted path turns off at right angles. From this point, the greater part of the approach route to Helvellyn can be prospected: a conspicuous gap in a wall-corner at the top left end of a large enclosure is the next objective. This gap is a mile and a half distant and 1500 ft higher, and obviously will require much time and collar-work to attain. In fact, most of the climbing on the walk occurs within this steep enclosure on the flank of Birkhouse Moor, the unremitting ascent being compensated by impressive views throughout of the upper reaches of Grisedale deeply confined by St Sunday Crag and Dollywaggon Pike.

The signposted path crosses Grisedale Beck by a bridge and starts the steep ascent beyond. At a junction of paths, the route continues uphill half left to a zigzag, where it turns right: this is an old pony track and drove-road for sheep, well graded and a pleasure to walk upon. At the corner of the first zigzag, another track going off to the left is a post-war variation created by impatient walkers wanting a more direct line to the gap. For many years, this modern alternative was pounded by boots until it fell apart in a landslip of boulders and scree, loose and dangerous and making an ugly scar on the fellside; walkers are now requested not to use this newer track. The pony route fell into disuse during these years but is incomparably better underfoot than the short cuts adopted by clumsy walkers. The men who laid its course long ago knew what they were doing; there is a lesson here for the beeline walkers of today. The pony route continues to climb in gentle curves and then aims directly for the gap.

Excitement mounts as the gap in the wall is passed through: there is a feeling that great things are ahead although as yet not fully in view. Gradually the path rises along the crest of steepening cliffs on the left and reaches the foot of an abrupt tower of rock. This has the name of High Spying How but is rarely referred to as such: to walkers coming this way it is the start of Striding Edge.

High Spying How

On my first visit here, as a raw apprentice on the hills and never having climbed a mountain before, and with a cousin equally bereft of experience, an eerie happening gave us a bad fright. We had set forth from Patterdale determined to see Striding Edge, having read much about it. Driving rain started as we climbed out of Grisedale but we went on hoping it would abate, which it never did. Soon we were enveloped in thick mist and soaked to the skin; there were no weather-protective anoraks and over-trousers in those days. We found the gap and went on along the crest, seeing nothing but a few yards of ground at our feet. Then suddenly there was a window in the mist and before us loomed a giant apparition, black as night: the uppermost rocks of the tower, its base remaining hidden so that it appeared as some threatening monster in the sky. We summoned a shred of courage and went on, traversing Striding Edge without seeing it and in due course arrived at the wall-shelter on Helvellyn.

In clear weather, the dark tower of High Spying How, although still impressive, has no terrors, and a distinct path climbing round its flank brings Striding Edge underfoot and a thrilling prospect ahead.

Striding Edge was long regarded as a fearful place to be avoided and in icy conditions or gale force winds can be frightening indeed and quite dangerous. It is Helvellyn's most dramatic feature: a narrow ridge of naked rock, a succession of jagged fangs high above and between very steep and shattered cliffs. The traverse can be made difficult or easy according to choice: an experienced scrambler on rocks will prefer to make his way along the very crest, but ordinary walkers will use a simple path running alongside a few feet below. In calm weather, this is an exhilarating adventure with an awkward drop at the far end the only hazard. The Edge is about 300 yards in length and so fascinating that one is tempted to go back and do it again. In modern times, Striding Edge has become the highlight in the itineraries of countless walkers who, in summer, have to travel in procession along it; there are even reports of people having to queue to get on it. There is an iron monument on the Edge that may be passed unnoticed: this is the Dixon Memorial, erected in 1858 to mark the scene of a fatal fall during a fox-hunt. The Dixons of those days seem to have been accident-prone; another Dixon fell to his death from the rim of Bleawater Crag on High Street.

Striding Edge and Helvellyn

(Opposite) Looking down Striding Edge from Helvellyn; (above) The summit of Helvellyn

Having safely negotiated the awkward chimney that terminates Striding Edge, a steep climb on a badly eroded path leads to easy ground on Helvellyn's broad and grassy top, the point of arrival thereon being at Gough's Memorial, erected in 1890 to commemorate a fatal accident in 1803. Charles Gough was a Kendal man out for a walk with his dog when he was killed by a fall from Striding Edge. Three months went by before his body was found with his faithful dog standing guard by the side of his dead master. The incident was widely reported and both Wordsworth and Scott wrote poems about it, dwelling more on the fidelity of the dog than on poor Gough. It is testimony to the infrequency of mountain ascents in those early days that three months should elapse before the discovery of the corpse.

It is now merely a short stroll to a cross-wall built as a shelter from wind and the summit is a few steps beyond; it might have been expected that the highest point would accommodate a massive cairn, but such is not the case, due no doubt to the paucity of suitable stones lying around. There is another memorial nearby at the top of the Wythburn path, a small tablet recording the landing of an aeroplane on Helvellyn by Bert Hinkler in 1926.

From the summit a magnificent all-round panorama presents itself.

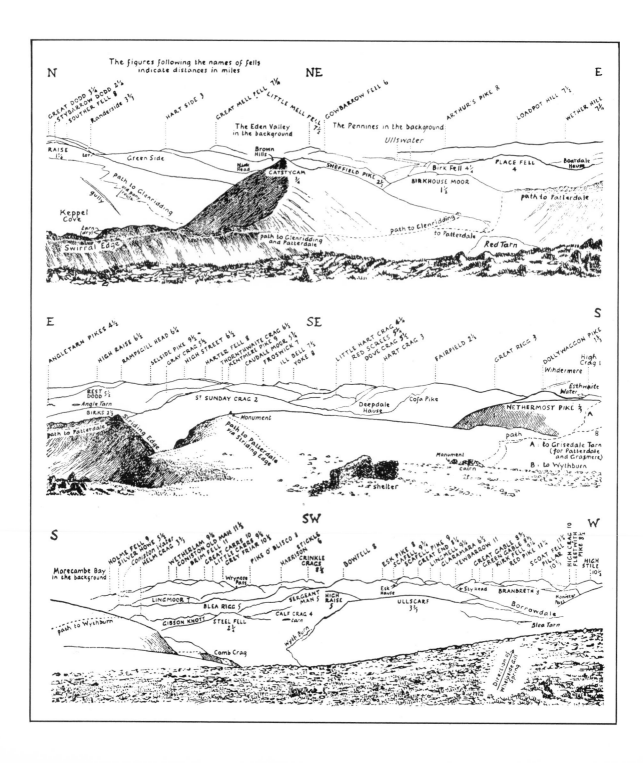

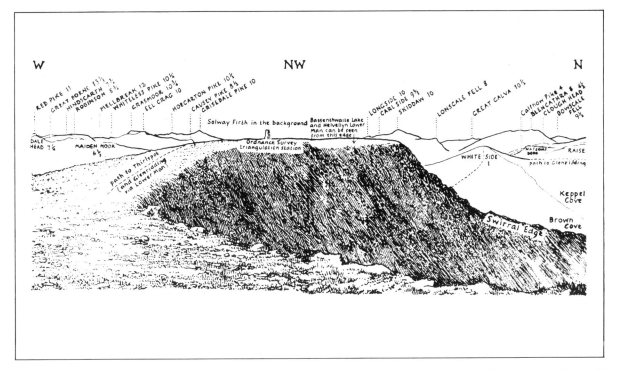

Continuing the story of my first visit with a cousin, Helvellyn now provided a mystery I was not to solve until the chance came for a second visit in the following year but which puzzled me greatly in the meantime. Our aim was Thirlspot, and both the Ordnance Survey and Bartholomew's maps showed only a pony route descending from Helvellyn's Lower Man and rising over the next fell, White Side, before finally coming down alongside Fisher Gill to Thirlspot. Still in pouring rain and with no visibility, we left the summit on a distinct and much-used path in the right direction, north, having no doubt that this was the promised pony route. Doubts began to arise, however, as our path continued to go down, directly and purposefully, with no sign of a rise to the top of White Side. Which path were we following, then, and where did it go? We were obviously off course, but went on, ever downwards, until emerging from the mist with Thirlspot below us.

On my second visit, in clear weather, I went up by the pony route charted on the maps, finding it difficult to trace, totally neglected, and intermittent over long distances. I came down by the blazed trail to Thirlspot as on the previous occasion. It was then clear to me that the pony route had been abandoned in favour of this newer and shorter way, which became known as the White Stones route. But not for many years thereafter was it acknowledged officially by inclusion on maps. To round off the story: we tramped to Keswick in sluicing rain and presented ourselves, two very sodden wretches, for a night's lodging at a boarding house. We were admitted by the lady of the house, each given a complete change of outfit from the husband's wardrobe, and royally fed, and in the morning our clothes were returned to us dry, warm and ironed. I mention this as an example of the concern and hospitality I was later to find typical of all the places, boarding houses, cottages and farms, where I had overnight stays in the district.

The next objective on the walk is Swirral Edge which, unlike Striding Edge, is steeply downhill. It is not seen from Helvellyn's summit and can be missed. To reach it, skirt the edge of the north-eastern cliffs where there is a sensational view of Red Tarn in a stony basin below, pass a triangulation column, and two minutes further, an obvious path descends a breach in the crags with the ground falling away sharply on both sides. This is Swirral Edge. The way down is eroded and slippery: two accidents have occurred here recently, one in snowy conditions and proving fatal.

At the foot of Swirral Edge, the path continues down to the outlet of Red Tarn, but straight ahead along a rising ridge is the shapely peak of Catstycam, 2917 ft, also known as Catchedicam and meaning Wild Cat's Hill, and a deviation to its small and neat summit is recommended before going down to the tarn. It is a wonderfully airy perch, the ground on three sides falling away out of sight almost at once, and has a retrospective view of the imposing cliffs of Helvellyn and the steep declivity of Swirral Edge. Then, returning down the ridge, the path down to Red Tarn can be resumed. The outlet is forded and the facing slope ascended to regain the gap in the wall used on the approach from Grisedale, thus completing the circuit of the Edges.

Catstycam from Swirral Edge

(Above) Helvellyn and Swirral Edge from Catstycam; (below) Helvellyn and Red Tarn

From the gap in the wall, the pony route may be used to reverse the line of ascent on the outward journey and is a very pleasant way down into Grisedale, but this means retracing steps for the last two miles. If time permits, a more interesting alternative, affording lovely views of Ullswater and involving little extra climbing, is available by following the top side of the wall across the higher reaches of Birkhouse Moor and then descending to a depression containing Lanty's Tarn in a beautiful setting amongst trees.

Lanty's Tarn

Ullswater from Keldas

A short rise beyond Lanty's Tarn leads to the cairn on an abrupt wooded height known as Keldas which, although of modest altitude, is one of the finest viewpoints in Lakeland, a place where artists and photographers suffer paroxysms of joy. The views of Ullswater, framed between lovely pines, are superb. Keldas is deservedly a very popular resort of sojourners at Patterdale and Glenridding, offering rewards out of all proportion to the ease of ascent.

Descent from Keldas on the side overlooking Ullswater is definitely out of bounds, the slope being very steep, craggy and densely wooded. It is necessary to return to Lanty's Tarn and from there take a grassy trod south to the junction of paths met on the outward journey, there going down to the bridge over Grisedale Beck and so happily back to Patterdale; a perfect end to a perfect day, with a memory of Striding Edge that will never fade.

5 BLENCATHRA
FROM THRELKELD   (6 MILES)

Blencathra from the east

A few decades ago, Blencathra seemed to be in danger of losing its lovely Celtic name in favour of the more prosaic Saddleback, which many writers who wrote about it (including Baddeley) and many walkers who walked on it appeared to prefer, their justification for doing so being the mountain's high skyline when seen from the east, a depression on the ridge between the summit and Foule Crag suggesting a saddle. The Ordnance Survey, to their credit, have not been influenced to abandon the old name but give both versions on their maps, naming the mountain as 'Saddleback or Blencathra'. I would be better pleased with 'Blencathra or Saddleback'. Happily the old name has been revived and is again in common use. There are many saddlebacks on the fells, named and unnamed. But only one Blencathra.

(Opposite) Blencathra from Castlerigg Stone Circle

Blencathra is one of the grandest mountains in Lakeland and the most imposing of all. It stands in isolation, is strongly individualistic and of unique character. It compels attention even from those people whose eyes are not habitually lifted to the hills. Its supreme feature, the one that endows it with special grandeur, is the very impressive southern front, a remarkable example of the effect of elemental natural forces. This flank forms a tremendous façade above the valley of the Greta, making a dark and towering backcloth to the emerald fields and woodlands, the cottages and farms along its base. There is nothing inviting in these shattered cliffs and petrified rivers of stone that seem to hold a perpetual threat over the community of Threlkeld and the surrounding countryside: the scene is awesome, intimidating and repelling. Few who gaze upon these desolate heights that leap so dramatically into the sky are likely to feel any inclination to venture into their arid, stony wildernesses and scramble up to the serrated summit ridge so high above. Consequently the area has remained a no-man's-land for walkers even though within close sight of the main road below. Blencathra is a popular ascent and climbed thousands of times a year but rarely by ways directly up the southern front, which is a pity for here is the greatness of the mountain, here are its more intimate aspects, and they make a fascinating study.

The outer slopes, rising on the west and east flanks from valley level to the uppermost escarpment fringing the summit ridge, are smoothly curved, massive and yet so symmetrical that they might well have been designed by a master architect to supply a perfect balance to the structure. These two outliers are Blease Fell and Scales Fell.

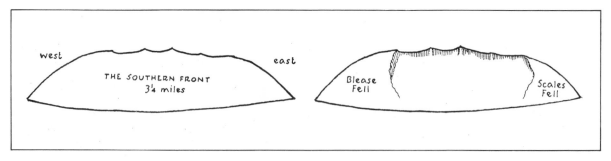

From their extremities, the slopes of Blease Fell and Scales Fell extend uneventfully towards each other across the front until suddenly and dramatically halted at the edge of a scene of devastation, the wreckage of what appears to have been, in ages past, a tremendous convulsion that tore the heart out of the mountain and left the ruins seemingly in a state of tottering collapse. The scene is chaotic: a great upheaval of ridges and pinnacles springing out of dead wastes of scree and penetrated by choked gullies and ravines, the whole crazily tilted through an altitude of 2,000 ft. Even in this area of confusion and disorder, however, Nature has fashioned a distinct pattern.

Four watercourses emerge from the surrounding debris to escape to the valley. Between the four ravines, three lofty spurs, similar in their characteristics, thrust far out, narrow and frail where they leave the main mass of the mountain but widening into substantial buttresses as they descend to the valley. It is as though a giant hand has clawed at the mountain, each finger scooping out a deep hollow with narrow strips of ground left undisturbed between.

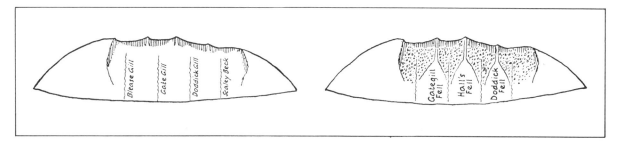

There are thus five buttresses on the southern front, each named as a separate fell. The two outer ones are grassy and have flat tops; the three in the middle are heathery and rise to distinct peaks, the central one being Blencathra's summit.

Such is the pattern of the southern front of Blencathra.

I spent all my leisure time in the winter of 1960-1 exploring Blencathra, thinking about it and writing about it. I climbed all the five ridges and struggled up the four scree-filled watercourses that so deeply divide them. I became familiar with every detail of the topography, scrambling over rough ground where surely no man had trod before, and was completely fascinated by its many ramifications. Never, on any of these wanderings, did I see another person and not even a sheep. This was a no-man's-land in very truth, a steep and inhospitable wilderness, yet, looking down, I could see the busy road only a mile away. I developed a great liking for Blencathra. Familiarity did not bring contempt, only admiration and affection.

Of the nine possible routes of ascent from the south, positively the best is Hall's Fell. This has all the attributes of a perfect climb. It is direct, exhilarating, has glorious views and, especially satisfying, scores a bull's eye by leading unerringly to the summit cairn. This is my favourite way up Blencathra.

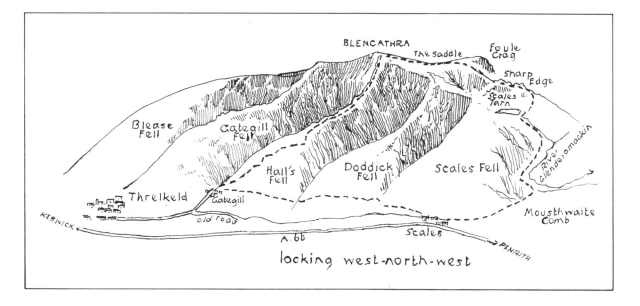

looking west-north-west

Threlkeld is now bypassed by a broad highway, the revised A66, happily for the inhabitants although its planned continuation through the outskirts of Keswick aroused much abortive opposition from outdoor associations concerned that the gentle beauty of the Lake District should not be scarred by the works of man.

Hall's Fell, named after Threlkeld Hall in the valley below it, is reached by following the old road through the village eastwards and turning up a lane on the left to Gategill, once a centre of lead-mining activity and having the kennels of the Blencathra Foxhounds adjacent, but now a scene of devastation, the debris of the mine intermingling with stones fallen into the narrow confines of the gill from the towering slopes on both sides. When an intake wall turns away on the right, the open fell is reached above it and an enchanting track winds upwards through the heather, enchanting because it cannot be seen from below and is revealed ahead only a few yards at a time, beckoning irresistibly up the broad base of the fell to the exciting ridge above. As height is gained, the fell narrows to a crest known locally as Narrow Edge and with good reason, and from here onwards the walk is delectable, threading a way amongst low crags and rocky steps and gateways and towers. A thin track on grass avoids all difficulties, but this is no place for travelling at speed: care is needed especially at one awkward spot where a rockface has to be traversed along a horizontal crack. But it is all quite delightful and the views down into the deep ravines on both sides are sensational.

Then the ridge, still well defined, rises sharply to the top of the fell, arriving there precisely at a heap of stones marking the highest point of Blencathra, at 2847 ft. With labours over for the time being, a splendid panorama can be enjoyed, the view between south and west being particularly good and crowded with detail.

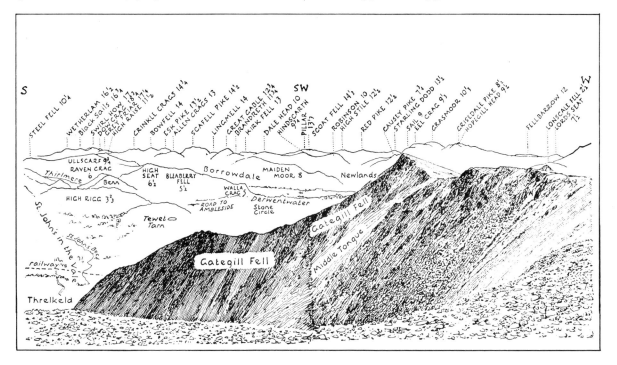

(Opposite) Narrow Edge looking up to Blencathra

The summit of Blencathra

Samuel T. Coleridge wrote of the summit:

> On stern Blencathra's perilous height
> The winds are tyrannous and strong . . .

but, although steep declivities fall away very sharply, there are no perils for those who walk circumspectly; and there are gentle breezes as well as strong winds, and soft couches for sunbathing. Blencathra isn't a monster.

The walk continues, now on excellent turf, in the direction of Foule Crag, seen due north, and descends easily to the saddle that inspired the naming of the mountain as Saddleback. Here in the depression is a landmark that has aroused the curiosity of visitors for many years: a collection of white crystallised stones of high quartz content laid on the ground in the form of a cross. This cross owes its existence to the industry of a Threlkeld man, Harold Robinson. Originally there was a very small cross of stones here (locally ascribed as a memorial to a walker who lost his life by a fall nearby), and Mr Robinson, an enthusiastic hill wanderer who has climbed his favourite mountain, Blencathra, hundreds of times, collected more stones (veins of quartzite occur in the native slate around) and extended the cross to its present size of 16 ft by 10 ft during a succession of visits from 1945 onwards. A much smaller but similar white cross on the southern slope of the saddle is more recent and the work of persons unknown.

(Below) The white cross   *(Opposite) Sharp Edge*

The next objective is Sharp Edge, which can be seen jutting from the steep slope on the right. A river of stones, formerly a path, leads steeply down to a narrow neck or col connecting the Edge with the mountain. Its aspect is intimidating; to the pioneer walkers of the last century, it was a place of terror. An early visitor, a Mr Green, described his passage along Sharp Edge as follows:

> We had not gone far before we were aware that our journey would be attended with perils; the passage gradually grew narrower and the declivity on each hand awfully precipitous. From walking erect we were reduced to the necessity either of bestriding the ridge or of moving on one of its sides with our hands lying over the top, as a security against falling into the tarn or into a frightful gully, both of immense depth. Sometimes we thought it prudent to return, but this seemed unmanly, and we proceeded, thinking with Shakespeare that 'dangers retreat when boldly they're confronted'.

Sharp Edge is even narrower than Striding Edge on Helvellyn, the crest in places being a razor-edge and the crags falling from it near vertical. But, like Striding Edge, a pedestrian path accompanies the crest a few feet below it on the north side and is without difficulty except for an initial problem where a sloping slab is negotiated by shuffling along it in a sitting position. Sharp Edge is much shorter than Striding Edge, and at the far end the path turns steeply down to the tarn mentioned by Mr Green, Scales Tarn, which is situated so far from Sharp Edge that he could not possibly have fallen into it.

Scales Tarn

Scales Tarn occupies a lonely basin shadowed by craggy heights. Sir Walter Scott refers to it thus in his *Bridal of Triermain:*

> Never sunbeam could discern
> The surface of that sable tarn,
> In whose black mirror you may spy
> The stars, while noontide lights the sky.

These words are well larded with poetic licence. I have sat in warm sunshine by Scales Tarn, and never have I seen stars reflected on the surface of the water in daylight. Of interest are lava deposits in the vicinity.

(Left) Doddick Gill ; (right) Scaley Beck

From the outlet of the tarn, a path descends into the valley of the River Glenderamackin and continues distinctly above the river until departing from it to climb over a low col into Mousthwaite Comb and so reach the hamlet of Scales, where there is an inn, the White Horse. Here the A66 can be joined for a quick return to Threlkeld; where the old road can be used, it should be: it is quiet, pleasant and tree-shaded. But to many fellwalkers, tramping on tarmac is anathema, and these may find a way back to Gategill on grass by keeping above the intake walls from Scales, this route giving intimate views of Scaley Beck and Doddick Gill in deep ravines, both crossed on the way.

Threlkeld offers rest and refreshment and those who do this walk will feel a need for both. But they will have had a grand day, and it is not unlikely that they will share my affection, not for Saddleback but for Blencathra.

6 SKIDDAW
FROM RAVENSTONE (6 MILES)

Skiddaw is the fourth highest mountain in Lakeland, one of the noblest in appearance, and the first to take shape when the landscape was being formed by convulsions of Nature.

It would be a gross exaggeration to say that Skiddaw is to Keswick what the Matterhorn is to Zermatt, but there is a certain affinity. Both are mountains of distinction, both are commanding heights dominating the valleys below, both are magnets that catch the eye whenever seen and draw the feet towards them, both are greatly loved by those who are privileged to live in their company. But there the analogy ends.

Skiddaw is not a detached peak soaring high into the sky; on the contrary, it is the centre-piece of a group, its summit magnificently buttressed by a circle of lesser heights, all of them proud members of the Skiddaw family, the whole forming a splendid and complete example of mountain structure especially well seen from all directions because of its isolation. Its outlines are smooth, its curves graceful, but because the slopes are steep everywhere, the quick build-up of the massif from valley levels to central summit is appreciated at a glance – and it should be an appreciative glance, for such massive strength and such beauty of outline rarely go together. Here, on Skiddaw, they do.

Skiddaw is the oldest of the Lakeland mountains according to the evidence of its rocks. It is apparent, even to unobservant walkers, that the stones covering the summit and exposed in eroded gullies and watercourses are very different in character from those seen in the central part of the Lake District: the latter are of volcanic origin, those on Skiddaw are marine deposits and consist in the main of soft shales and slate that splits readily into thin wafers and soon crumbles and decays when exposed to the atmosphere; hence it has no commercial value.

Skiddaw was formed long before the volcanos of central Lakeland became active; later it overlooked a vast glacier system, a world of ice. Some volcanic boulders are found along the lower southern slopes of the Skiddaw group: these rocks have been identified with those of the cliffs enclosing St John's Vale, having been carried along and deposited here when the glaciers retreated and scoured the flanks of Skiddaw on their way to the frozen sea.

Skiddaw is a giant in stature, but an affable and friendly giant. And a benevolent one. Keswick people have an inborn affection for Skiddaw, and it is well earned. The mountain makes a great contribution to the scenic beauty of the Vale of Keswick, shelters it from northerly gales, supplies it with pure water, feeds its sheep, and provides a recreation ground for its visitors. Throughout the centuries, Skiddaw's beacon has warned of impending troubles and alarms – 'the red glare on Skiddaw roused the burghers of Carlisle' – and today shares in Keswick's rejoicings.

Skiddaw and Keswick are inseparable.

(Opposite) Skiddaw from Ashness Bridge

Skiddaw from the boat landings on Derwentwater

Before the district was invaded by motor cars and the more remote mountains thus made more accessible, Skiddaw was the mountain most often climbed, Keswick then having a convenient railway service. The ascent of Skiddaw was the highlight of a visit to Keswick and almost a tradition. The top was regularly attained on the backs of ponies, refreshments being available at a hut midway. Not all who did the climb enjoyed the experience: there are reports of visitors being struck with horror at the sight of the steep declivities falling from their feet, of others wishing to lose blood and return to the safe ground below. But the ascent was the manly thing to do for sojourners at Keswick, an epic performance, and all went up the same way, on pony or on foot; a beaten track came into being designed to ease the passage of ponies. At that time, this was the only route to the summit and it is still today by far the most popular, often crowded with earnest pedestrians many of whom are unaware of any other.

All mountain climbs are worth the effort, but it must be admitted that the tourist path, starting from the back of Latrigg (Skiddaw's cub) is tedious and unexciting. Infinitely to be preferred is the route I like to follow, up and over the Ullock Pike ridge to the west, high above Bassenthwaite Lake: it is an exhilarating expedition, quiet and unfrequented, and has excellent views throughout.

The walk starts from the Ravenstone Hotel, between Little Crosthwaite and High Side on the Carlisle road out of Keswick, where a gated lane alongside the hotel grounds, with Dodd Wood on the right, leads steeply up to the open fell. Ullock Pike is now seen towering over rough, craggy and uninviting slopes that rule out a direct ascent. To circumvent this difficulty, turn left above an intake wall, away from Ullock Pike, and make a great loop to reach the ridge, known as the Edge, from which the summit springs. Already there is a pleasing prospect of Bassenthwaite Lake below the line of approach and an impressive view down into Southerndale on the east side. On the ridge below will be seen a strange group of boulders, Watches, which will be visited on the return journey. Now every step is a joy. The Edge rises ahead and is followed over minor undulations on a thin track amid heather, with sensational views into the depths of Southerndale as height is gained. The sharp peak of Ullock Pike, looking like a baby Matterhorn, soars ahead and is duly reached after passing over a false summit. The highest point, at 2230 ft, is a delectable spot, a place to linger amongst comfortable heather couches, and enjoy magnificent views. Skiddaw is now prominent and the route to it over the next summit, Long Side, can be traced, but it is Bassenthwaite Lake far below that most arrests the attention. The large scale Ordnance maps show a Hanging Stone on the nearby crags but this is not worth the search, being merely an unremarkable rock anchored to the lip of a small cliff. It is with reluctance that one leaves the airy perch of this lovely summit; it is the sort of place to make one wish it could be parcelled up and taken home for the back garden. It is delightful. All worldly troubles vanish on the top of Ullock Pike.

The Edge, Ullock Pike

Ullock Pike from Chapel hamlet

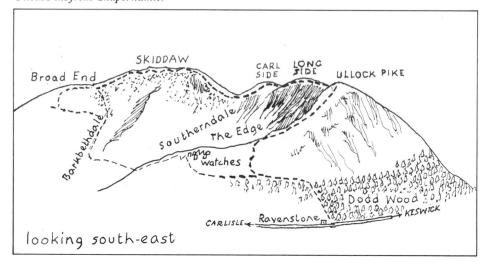

Broad End · SKIDDAW · CARL SIDE · LONG SIDE · ULLOCK PIKE

Barkbethdale · Southerndale · The Edge · watches · Dodd Wood

CARLISLE ← Ravenstone · KESWICK

looking south-east

From Ullock Pike, the walk continues along the crest of a well-defined ridge named Longside Edge, with startling glimpses down the shattered cliffs falling into the depths of Southerndale. At one point, a cleft cuts into the ridge but there is no rock to handle and an easy rise leads to the top of Long Side, 2405 ft. This summit is also very pleasant, a carpet of dry moss, heather and bilberry tempting another halt. Strictly this summit is nameless, Long Side properly being the broad western flank, the lower slopes of which are densely afforested.

From the top of Long Side, a narrow trod descends to the depression before Carl Side, and a grassy beeline may be made for its summit at 2420 ft, or it may be bypassed by a more direct track to the tiny Carlside Tarn and the col that connects Carl Side to a broad shoulder of Skiddaw.

(Right, above) The summit of Ullock Pike, looking to Long Side; (right) The summit of Long Side, looking across to Ullock Pike; (below) From Carl Side, looking to Skiddaw

Carlside Col is a high neck of land, with Southerndale going steeply down on the left and a stony ravine descending on the right. There are interesting formations around where the slate bedrock breaks the surface. Rising ahead is a shoulder of Skiddaw, littered with loose shale and scree that makes the ascent arduous. Relief from effort is obtained on easier ground above where a cairn marks the south top of Skiddaw at an elevation of 3034 ft. Here the popular tourist path is joined and parties of human beings may be expected. The view south from this point is quite beautiful but better still is the comprehensive panorama seen from Skiddaw Little Man, prominent half a mile down the tourist path, where the outlook over Derwentwater and Borrowdale to the central heights of Lakeland is superb. I consider this viewpoint to be the finest in the district.

Long Side and Ullock Pike with Carlside Col in the foreground

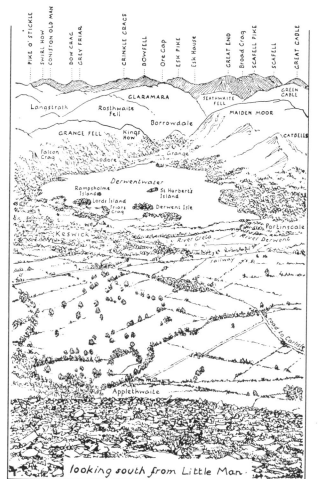

looking south from Little Man

The summit of Skiddaw

The top of Skiddaw is in the form of an undulating ridge exceeding 3000 ft throughout its length of almost half a mile, providing an easy promenade and a rare feeling of freedom and escape from the world far below and, for a time, quite forgotten.

There is a south top and a north top, a middle top and a main top, all in a straight line and connected by stony pavements. In mist, it is not uncommon to assume that the middle top is the highest, there being a fall in the ground beyond, but the true summit, at 3054 ft, is further along and has a triangulation column.

Skiddaw is often described as 'merely a grassy hill', but its airy summit is the summit of a mountain. It commands a far-reaching view, north to the Solway Firth and the hills of Galloway, west to the sea, east to the Pennines and south to Lakeland, the principal fells being arrayed in a great arc between east and west. Walkers who have been to the Isle of Man will be pleased to see it again.

One evening during the early years of the war, I went up Skiddaw at dusk to spend the night on the summit, finding the blackness illumined by a strange red glow in the sky to the south; next day came the news that Liverpool had been bombed.

From the north top, and again out of sight and sound of other human beings, the walk goes on in the same direction, down the descending ridge to a col, with the profound hollow of Barkbethdale far below on the left, and a way down into that valley may be made from this point on a steep and stony slope. Or, alternatively, to avoid rough ground, the walk may be continued to Broad End, there descending grassy slopes on the left to reach a drove-road or sledgate that enters Barkbethdale at a lower level. This valley is quiet and unfrequented except by sheep, and almost unknown except to the shepherds of Barkbeth Farm. The sledgate leads distinctly to an intake wall and this should be followed to the left into the next valley, Southerndale, where the grimmer aspects of Ullock Pike and Long Side are revealed.

Barkbethdale

(Above) Southerndale; (below, right) Watches

Southerndale Beck is crossed by a footbridge and the facing slope climbed to renew acquaintance with the Edge at its lower part and here will be found the strange group of boulders known as Watches, huddled together as if assembled in conference and suggesting, at first sight, a Druids' Circle. The formation is natural, however, but unusual and, being in a vast expanse of grass, unexpected. The name of Watches given to it on large-scale Ordnance maps, is no less intriguing.

Without having solved the mystery of Watches, the intake wall followed in the early part of the walk is quickly reached down the west slope, and by turning left alongside it, the lane going down to Ravenstone returns the walker to the main Keswick–Carlisle road and his parked car; or, if without one, a regular bus service is available.

7 THE LANGDALE PIKES
FROM GREAT LANGDALE   (6 MILES)

There are many mountains in Lakeland with such a distinctive outline that they are instantly identifiable on sight by most visitors to the district, but no mountain profile arrests and excites the attention more than that of the Langdale Pikes, nor is more well known by name, nor is more easily recognisable. To travellers on the road alongside Windermere, to those who sail on the waters of the lake or picnic on its shores, their abrupt outline has a dramatic appeal not shared by higher mountains within the range of view. Even visitors whose itineraries go no further than the pier at Waterhead, and the many who think that all mountains look alike, know the group by name and proudly and loudly announce it to their company. The Langdale Pikes cannot be ignored.

The distant view from Windermere is impressive, but when the Pikes are seen more intimately on the approach along the lovely valley of Great Langdale they become imposing indeed, even awesome, leaping from the flat pastures in a tremendous upsurge that stirs the imagination and even the emotions, and most especially whenever the towering peaks come into view suddenly and unexpectedly. The difference in altitude between top and base is little more than 2000 ft yet, because it occurs in a lateral distance of only three-quarters of a mile, it is enough to convey a remarkable impression of remoteness and inaccessibility to the craggy summits surmounting the rugged slopes.

(Opposite) Langdale Pikes from Lingmoor Fell

There are five summits in the group, extending in an arc and all overtopping the steep Langdale flank. In the order of their appearance from the west they are Pike o' Stickle, Loft Crag, Thorn Crag, Harrison Stickle and Pavey Ark.

Pike o' Stickle and Loft Crag

The usual route of ascent from Great Langdale is much trodden, and every turn and twist of the ingenious and circuitous path has been faithfully followed by generations of walkers. But it is unremittingly steep and on most days over-populated by the red and orange blobs of aspiring and perspiring climbers and littered by the recumbent bodies of those who have fallen by the wayside. Its one virtue is that it is as direct as the rough ground permits, but for walkers wishing to visit all five summits it has the disadvantage of arriving amongst them midway so that some untidy retracing of steps is necessary.

Whenever I have a choice between a steep path and an easy one I prefer the latter, and if it takes me on a roundabout course and is longer in distance so much the better: less effort will be entailed and more will be seen on the way.

For years I had walked along Mickleden from Great Langdale without ever being aware of a zigzag path up the west bank of Troughton Beck and in fact it cannot be traced from below. I am indebted to the Ordnance Survey for indicating this path on the 1901 edition of their six-inch map. It is an old drove-road, engineered for bringing sheep down to the valley, and is omitted from modern versions of their maps. I never saw anyone using it. This route is quiet, unencumbered with red and orange blobs, calls for less collar-work than the popular path, and has the advantage of arriving at one end of the five summits so that they can be visited one after another in a continuous traverse without deviations and back-tracking. This is the way I like to go.

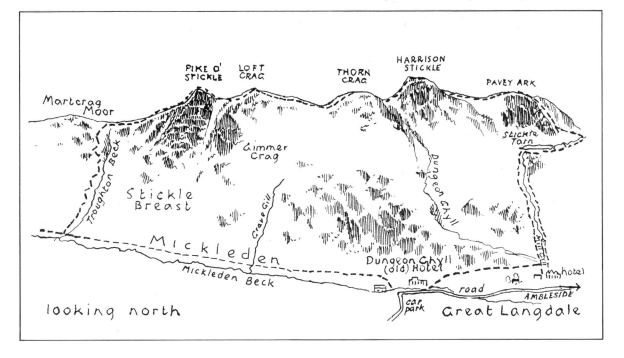

The walk starts from the old Dungeon Ghyll Hotel or the car park nearby, and proceeds along the side-valley of Mickleden as if bound for Rossett Gill or Stake Pass, passing along the base of Loft Crag, identifiable by the great buttress of Gimmer Crag, and then below the formidable acclivities of Stickle Breast, rising in tiered crags to the neat dome of Pike o' Stickle towering above. Beyond, the watercourse of Troughton Beck comes down on the right and, on its far bank, although not readily seen, rises the zigzag drove-road, not in evidence at first but becoming clear when the ground steepens. It is a long climb through 1400 ft of altitude, but relieved by the impressive sight of the wild upper parts of Pike o' Stickle. When the zigzags end, easier ground is ahead and the plateau of Martcrag Moor is reached. Here it will be seen, with surprise, that the Pikes do not fall away sharply on their north side as is suggested by their bold appearance from the valley; on the contrary, the summits rise but little above a sprawling and rather drab moorland. Turning right, and keeping close to the Mickleden edge, the thimble-shaped top of Pike o' Stickle is soon reached by a simple scramble, the summit cairn, at 2323 ft, having a fine view forward to the dominating height of Harrison Stickle, the highest of the group. There is little scope for exploration on the top of Pike o' Stickle, the ground falling away in precipices on three sides. Loft Crag, seen ahead, is the next objective but cannot be reached by a beeline, the short scramble to Pike o' Stickle's summit being reversed and a descent then made to the head of a wide scree gully, a place both of repute and ill-repute.

Pike o' Stickle from Troughton Beck

(Above) Harrison Stickle; (below) Loft Crag and Harrison Stickle from Pike o'Stickle

Until the Lake District was discovered in the early 19th century by discerning travellers who sang its praises in so fulsome a manner that they were followed by an ever-increasing flood of tourists, it was a land apart, reached only by a few turnpikes, aloof and unaffected by major national events and contributing nothing worthy of record in the history books. True, there had been a skirmish in Rannerdale between the natives and the Norman invaders, but that incident was almost forgotten. There were no famous battles here; civil wars, the rise and fall of Parliaments, the founding of the British Empire – these were matters that changed nothing here amongst the mountains. The Industrial Revolution meant nothing to the sheep, although they did hear talk of a railway reaching Keswick. Life went on undisturbed as it had done for centuries. There had been Celts and Vikings here and their place names lived on, but all that was ages ago. History had little to do with the Lake District.

But if Lakeland lacks an exciting history, a chance discovery a few decades ago established that it had an unsuspected and quite remarkable pre-history, evidenced by the stone-axe 'factories' of Neolithic man. The head of a stone axe, perfectly fashioned and obviously man-made, was found in the scree gully falling from Pike o' Stickle, and a search revealed more, some of them imperfect and obviously discarded, but many in good condition. Excitement ran high amongst local archaeologists; enthusiastic searchers scoured the loose scree of the gully and the fells in the vicinity, discovering other axes and chipping sites in many places around Langdale and always on the same high contour. Proof was positive. Thousands of years ago, there had been an industry here for the manufacture of stone axes, and on so active a scale that Langdale is now established as the most important of such sites in the country.

The intrusion of a narrow vein of a very hard and durable stone in the volcanic rocks of Great Langdale, emerging on the surface along a high-level contour around the head of the valley, provided the material from which the prehistoric natives of the district fashioned their axes. Working sites have been located from Martcrag Moor to Harrison Stickle, but the screes of Pike o' Stickle have yielded the most prolific discoveries, and especially the south scree gully where many hundreds of specimens, originally rejected because of imperfections, have been collected in recent years. The really remarkable feature is not so much the presence of this particular stratum, nor the making of implements from it so long ago; the facts that most tax the imagination are, first, that the primitive inhabitants of Lakeland should have located such an insignificant geological fault and recognised its value and, second, that the plentiful evidences of their industry should have remained undisturbed and unnoticed throughout the ages until modern times.

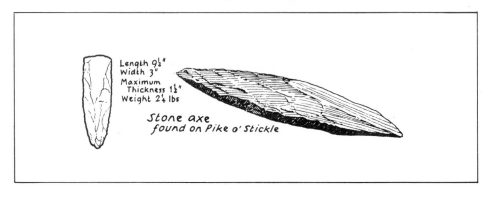

Length 9½"
Width 3"
Maximum
   Thickness 1½"
Weight 2¼ lbs

Stone axe
found on Pike o' Stickle

The scree gully has been so badly eroded by eager searchers of stone axes that it has become slippery and even dangerous, and walkers have been asked by the local Mountain Rescue Association to regard it as out of bounds. Before passing on, however, a man-made cave in the steep west wall of the gully is worthy of notice: its connection with stone-axe manufacture has not yet been accepted by learned archaeologists although the coincidence seems too great to be denied. It provides shelter for several persons.

Pike o'Stickle from Loft Crag

(Above) Langdale and Windermere from Harrison Stickle; (below) The upper ravine of Dungeon Ghyll

From the head of the gully there is a simple rise to the abrupt summit of Loft Crag, 2270 ft, an airy and pleasant top that has below it on the Langdale flank the imposing buttress of Gimmer Crag, a very popular resort of rock-climbers. The walk continues with an easy descent to another depression, this being crossed by the well-blazed tourist path. Rising beyond it is Thorn Crag, quickly ascended from this point and having nothing of special interest except an intimate view of the impending mass of Harrison Stickle, from which it is separated by a fearful chasm formed by the headwaters of Dungeon Ghyll. This hazard is avoided by descending the north slope of Thorn Crag rejoining the path for the final stiff pull up to Harrison Stickle.

I once spent an autumn night on this slope. I had walked up from the valley on a lovely evening and, having selected a bed in the heather, watched a fox on a grassy shelf below me, obviously enjoying life, playing and leaping and rolling like a ginger kitten, not knowing that he might be destined to be torn to pieces by dogs and that a brave hunter might cut off his tail for a trophy. Foxes, men say, are pests . . .

After darkness had fallen, a grey mist and a drizzling rain descended on the mountain. I had with me a khaki blanket, an Army reject, which served me well: there were posh sleeping bags in the shops but at a price beyond my pocket. In those days, I was rather addicted to spending nights out amongst the mountains. They were eerie vigils. The silence was absolute, the mountains were black silhouettes around me like crouching monsters. I was always too apprehensive to sleep and passed the long hours of darkness with a cigarette every thirty minutes. At sunrise, the mountains changed quickly from black to grey to rosy pink and welcomed me to their company. After my first such experience, I quite lost my fear of mountains; they became friends. The reason for this eccentric pastime, apart from wanting to feel myself part of the scene, was that it gave me a dawn start on the tops and a full day's walking and exploration ahead of me.

On this occasion when the first light of day filtered through the murk, I went up to the top of Harrison Stickle and quite suddenly and unexpectedly emerged from the mist and saw before me the summit rocks, stark and clear under a cloudless sky. I walked across to the Langdale cairn and was transfixed by the most beautiful scene I have ever witnessed. I was standing on an island in the midst of a sea of cotton wool that extended to the far horizon. Across the valley a few other peaks pierced the mist, also like islands rising from the sea, sharply defined but sullen in the half-light of dawn. I waited for the sun to rise. Gradually I felt the warmth of the first rays; the summit rocks became diffused with a soft pink glow and within minutes were bathed in sunshine and casting long shadows. There was a profound stillness in the air; down below the mist, I could hear a cock crowing at one of the Langdale farms, but there was no other sound, not even the whisper of a breeze. Then slowly the mist receded from the shoulders of the distant peaks and settled over the valleys. Langdale was completely filled by a white mist that extended from Rossett Pike at the dalehead and curved like an unbroken glacier, following the contours of the valley away into the distance over Elterwater and above the length of Windermere to the sea, a river of vapour, a mantle of unblemished purity. Alone I saw it; there were people down there in their beds who knew nothing of the glory of the morning. Still I waited. Very slowly the mist began to break, patches of green appeared, and within half an hour every vestige had dissipated, and I could see the fields of Langdale far below as on a map. The transformation was complete.

Harrison Stickle and Pavey Ark from across Langdale

The summit of Harrison Stickle, 2403 ft, takes the form of an elevated ridge supported by crags, the south side being precipitous. As befits the highest of the Pikes, the view commands the whole area and extends far into the distance. To the north is the last summit to be visited, Pavey Ark, the abrupt downfall of its great cliff being seen in profile.

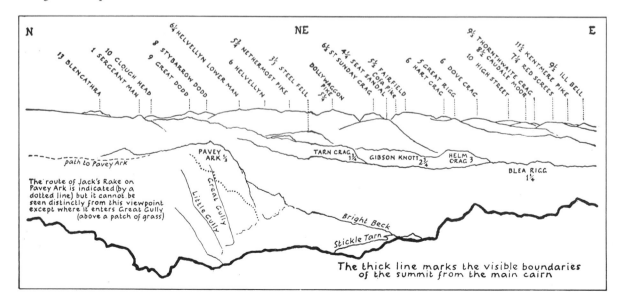

The route of Jack's Rake on Pavey Ark is indicated (by a dotted line) but it cannot be seen distinctly from this viewpoint except where it enters Great Gully (above a patch of grass)

The thick line marks the visible boundaries of the summit from the main cairn

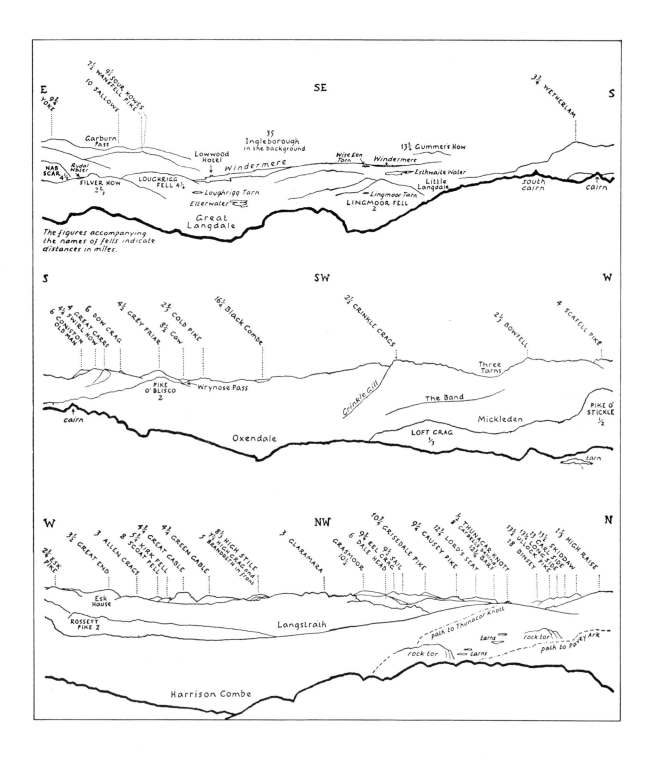

The figures accompanying the names of fells indicate distances in miles.

The way down from the summit of Harrison Stickle is initially rough and rocks have to be handled, but it is not difficult and soon reaches the grassy ridge leading up through outcrops to the top of Pavey Ark, 2288 ft. This is a delightful place: attractive grey rocks of a rough texture, not unlike the gabbro of Skye, are all around and interspersed with terraces of bilberry. Explorers should not wander too far from the cairn, the ground to the east falling in a tremendous plunge to the waters of Stickle Tarn far below: this is one of the greatest precipices in the district.

Pavey Ark from Harrison Stickle

Stickle Tarn is the next objective, but it is palpably obvious that there is no direct way down to it. The route continues beyond the cairn, keeping close to the edge of the crags until a wide grassy breach occurs on the right. This offers a remarkably simple escape from the fringe of rocks. I call it North Rake. As though cut out of the craggy surround by a knife, it leads straight down to the easy moorland below without hazards and with grass underfoot. An opening in the cliffs midway is better ignored: it leads into Easy Gully and debouches at the foot of the precipice but has a large chockstone which is awkward to negotiate.

At the lower end of North Rake, Bright Beck is crossed and followed downstream to its entry into Stickle Tarn, the walk continuing along the east bank of this large sheet of water. Now the cliffs of Pavey Ark are seen to great advantage, soaring into the sky in a broad and near-vertical wall of rock with channels of scree pouring from black clefts and gullies, the awesome grandeur of the scene enhanced by the dark waters of the tarn.

Pavey Ark from Stickle Tarn

Stickle Tarn has a dam, its waters formerly being impounded for the use of the gunpowder works at Elterwater, long gone. It is a popular excursion from Langdale, and from here down to the valley, parties of visitors must be expected. Issuing from the tarn is Mill Gill, in wet weather a cataract rather than a stream, and there are so-called paths on both banks going down to the valley; that on the west side is cut to ribbons of stones by over-use and that on the east side, once a thin track, suffers likewise by the pounding of boots. Both descend to the New Dungeon Ghyll Hotel and the valley road, but if the old hotel and the large car park is the destination, the intake wall can be followed to avoid almost a mile of road walking. Nobody ever climbs the Langdale Pikes without taking a last lingering look at them before leaving their magnificent presence.

8 CRINKLE CRAGS
FROM GREAT LANGDALE (8 MILES)

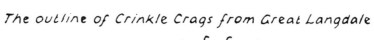

The outline of Crinkle Crags from Great Langdale

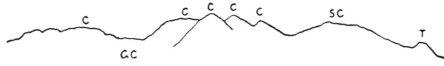

C : The five Crinkles   GC : Great Cove
T : Rock tower near Three Tarns   SC : Shelter Crags

The highest Crinkle (2816') is second from the left on the diagram.
When seen from the valley it does not appear to be the highest, as
it is set back a little from the line of the others.

A few of the fells of Lakeland have inherited their name from the Norse invaders of long ago, and these rough men must surely have had poetry in their souls for they have left us with Blencathra, Helvellyn, Glaramara and other romantic titles. Some fells have taken their names from communities in their vicinity, such as Coniston Old Man, Rosthwaite Fell and Glenridding Dodd. Some are named after the valleys from which they rise, Langdale Pikes, Bowscale Fell and Esk Pike being examples, and some, such as Watson's Dodd, Harrison Stickle and Robinson, owe their names to forgotten dalesmen. But most were named by the first settlers because of obvious physical characteristics, Great Gable, Red Pike, Steeple and Pillar amongst them.

In this latter category is the fell known as Crinkle Crags, so named by the early men of Langdale, an apt description for the serrated skyline seen from that valley: a succession of knobs and depressions distinguishing it from all others in the area. These undulations, seeming trivial at a distance, are revealed at close range as steep rocky buttresses and scree gullies above wild and arid slopes, the whole a scene of rugged grandeur.

Crinkle Crags has a special appeal for walkers who like rough ground underfoot without finding themselves in difficult situations. The full traverse of the five summits is an exciting adventure, a lofty promenade amidst rocky outcrops and boulders throughout, and with unsurpassed views down into Langdale and across to the Scafells and Bowfell. But in misty conditions it is easy to go astray, the path being intermittent in places and the terrain confusing. The company of Crinkle Crags should be sought only in clear and settled weather – then it is with reluctance that one says farewell at the end of an exhilarating day.

(Opposite) Crinkle Crags from Pike o'Blisco

The easiest route of ascent, if a car is available, is from Wrynose Pass where there are roadside parking spaces. This is a simple and straightforward walk with two great disadvantages: the tremendous Langdale flank is not seen in its full stature, and there is no convenient way back to the car except by reversing the line of approach.

The usual way from Great Langdale goes via Stool End Farm into the side valley of Oxendale, following the beck upstream for half a mile and then climbing steeply to pass over Brown How and so reach Red Tarn, where the path from Wrynose Pass is joined. This route is rather stuffy and does not disclose the Crinkles in their full glory: it is indicated on the diagram below but without recommendation.

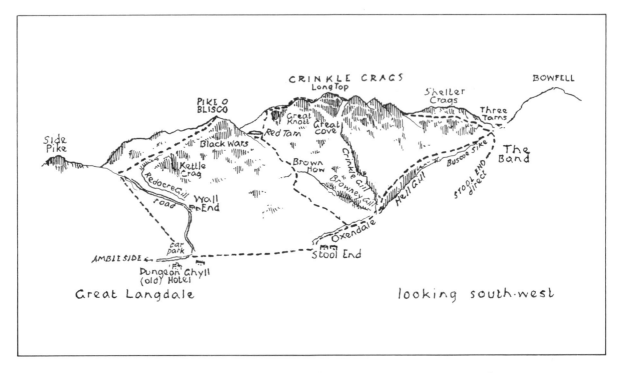

Unquestionably the finest way of reaching Crinkle Crags is, as a preliminary, to make the traverse of Pike o' Blisco en route for Red Tarn. This gives high-level walking throughout, with fine views of the Coniston fells and intimate glimpses down into the deepening gulf of Oxendale as height is gained, and from the summit the Crinkles are seen to perfection and in true perspective. The disadvantage of first visiting Pike o' Blisco is the considerable descent from its summit to Red Tarn, entailing about 500 ft of extra ups and downs, but this is a small price to pay for the pleasure of crossing the Pike, the additional effort being recompensed by its interesting summit and wonderful views. This is the route I shall describe.

The walk starts from the car park around the turn of the road near the old Dungeon Ghyll Hotel. A path goes straight up the slope of Side Pike and rejoins the road at its highest point. Here the open fell is gained and a track on the right leads above the ravine of Redacre Gill and the cliffs of Kettle Crag, rising gradually for a mile to the rocky top of Pike o' Blisco. This is a pleasant place and a colourful one, with pinky-grey rocks outcropping all around and interspersed by green mosses and dark heather. The summit cairn is grandly sited on a platform of naked rock at a height of 2304 ft. This is a splendid viewpoint, Bowfell and Crinkle Crags being especially well seen in their full majesty.

The summit was originally crowned by a tall and elegant cairn, a conspicuous and familiar landmark when viewed from Great Langdale. I always looked up at it when visiting that valley but there came an occasion in 1959 when it was missing from the scene. This was a shock: that fine column of stones, the work of a professional, had withstood the gales and storms for as long as I could recall. I went up to see what had happened and was dismayed to find the stones scattered on the ground. There was no doubt that the cairn had been deliberately thrown down. This was the first evidence I had that the vandals and wreckers had emerged from their urban haunts and found their way up the fells. Regular fellwalkers are conservationists and never commit wilful damage on the mountains; they like them exactly as they are. I issued an appeal for volunteers to rebuild the cairn and, bless them, they did. To pull down a summit cairn is sacrilege.

Summit cairn
Pike o' Blisco (pre-1959)

The summit of Pike o'Blisco

Crinkle Crags and Bowfell from Red Tarn

A good path descends from Pike o' Blisco to Red Tarn. I never like losing height that I know must be regained, nor do most fellwalkers, but in this instance the traverse of the Pike will have been enjoyed so much that there will be few grumbles.

Red Tarn is an unattractive sheet of water but not without merit on a hot day. It is a walkers' crossroads, four paths converging near the outlet.

Gladstone's Finger

From a small patch of red scree 100 yards below the outlet of Red Tarn the continuation of the route to Crinkle Crags climbs the grass slope to the west and is fairly steep until a prominent crag on the right, Great Knott, is rounded, when the gradient eases and the path heads directly for the first Crinkle, now in sight ahead. Here a diversion from the path is recommended, crossing to the right to the edge of the crags of Great Knott and following a parallel course until, at the top of a short scree gully, the remarkable pinnacle known as Gladstone's Finger is disclosed, rising out of a choke of stones: a slender monolith that has survived ages of weathering while much around it has disintegrated. Beyond this gully, and keeping on the same course, a dramatic view of the second and third Crinkles is revealed across the profound hollow of Great Cove. Then the path is resumed for the traverse of the first Crinkle, 2733 ft. This takes the form of a ridge, rough and rocky with many cairns to keep walkers on the right track; sheer cliffs make an abrupt edge to the ridge and there are sensational views down two gullies. The second (and highest and biggest) Crinkle is now ahead, appearing as a huge rocky dome.

The second Crinkle, from the first

The first Crinkle is descended at its far end to a grassy depression and an obvious scree gully is seen leading upwards to the top of the second Crinkle. Things are not as they seem, however; the gully, when entered, is found to be not at all an obvious route. Here is the Bad Step, the most difficult obstacle on any pedestrian path in the district: two chockstones block the gully entirely, forming a rocky wall ten feet high and as near vertical as makes no difference, and quite beyond the powers of the average walker to scale. To avoid this problem, it is usual to turn left at the depression and climb a wide grassy rake that leads to the summit of the second Crinkle, 2816 ft, which is named Long Top because of a high lateral spur going off westwards. Here the Scafell range comes suddenly into view across upper Eskdale and Bowfell appears ahead over a very bouldery foreground.

The Bad Step
from below

The Scafell range from Long Top

Bowfell from the third Crinkle

The next objective after Long Top is the third Crinkle, seen rising like a pyramid from a desert of stones. Walkers whose luck is in will find amongst the rocks on the initial stage of the descent from Long Top a most unexpected and welcome spring: it is the highest flow of water in the Lake District but only worth searching for after rain. A clear path goes down to the head of a wide scree gully known as Mickledoor and then skirts the base of the third Crinkle, a pathless scramble over boulders being necessary to reach its neat summit at 2740 ft. This has a fine view of Bowfell, seen over the fourth and fifth Crinkles, but the gem is the prospect of the green fields of Great Langdale in sharp contrast to the wilderness of stones all around.

The fourth and fifth Crinkles, next to be visited, are replicas of the third but of descending height. The path skirts both summits on the west side, gradually declining amongst a desolation of boulders and scree; grass is at a premium hereabouts. The top of the fourth, at 2730 ft, is only a few yards from the path and quickly attained. The top of the fifth, at 2680 ft, which is named Gunson Knott, is 20 yards from the path and reached by a scramble. These two minor summits, although encompassed by very rough ground, should not be by-passed: both are small domes formed by piled rocks and both have superlative views of Great Langdale.

Beyond the fifth Crinkle, the stones are left behind and normal walking can be resumed as the path passes over the shoulder of Shelter Crags and descends to the wide grassy depression of Three Tarns (actually there are four), below the huge façade of Bowfell, riven by a dozen parallel gullies known as the Links of Bowfell.

(Above) Bowfell from one of the Three Tarns   *(Opposite) Hell Gill and Whorneyside Force*

Three Tarns is another walkers' crossroads and much visited, usually during the ascent of Bowfell, and is a popular crossing between Eskdale and Great Langdale. The latter valley can be reached directly from here by way of a long descending shoulder of Bowfell, The Band, which has a good path down to Stool End.

But Crinkle Crags has not yet exhausted its surprises, and instead of returning to Great Langdale immediately, a much more interesting route follows the stream taking shape on the right, Buscoe Sike, which soon enters the deep chasm of Hell Gill. The bed of the gill is impassable but there is no difficulty in descending along the edge of the ravine, which in its lower reaches displays the waterfall of Whorneyside Force.

(Above) Crinkle Gill ; (below) Browney Gill

At the foot of Hell Gill the scenery is most spectacular. Crinkle Gill and Browney Gill join forces here in typical Wild West country, a meeting place of gulches and canyons and tumbling waters in very rough terrain devastated by rockfalls and landslips. Escape is provided by a path alongside the combined streams, hereon called Oxendale Beck, and Stool End is reached without further excitement. But before arriving at the farm, a look back reveals again the five Crinkles, aloof and seemingly unattainable, that have given such an enjoyable adventure and made the day so memorable.

Crinkle Crags from Oxendale

9 BOWFELL AND ESK PIKE
FROM GREAT LANGDALE   (8 MILES)

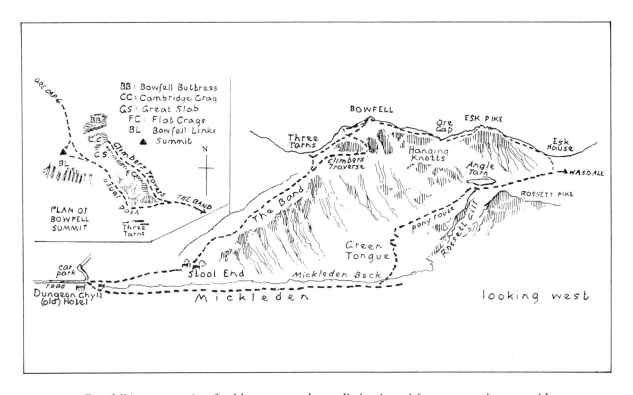

Bowfell is a mountain of noble aspect and rare distinction, rising as a massive pyramid at the head of three lovely valleys, Great Langdale, Eskdale and Langstrath, and commanding attention whenever it appears in a view. Shapeliness and sturdiness do not always go together but here on Bowfell they do. The higher the slopes rise from their sprawling base the rougher they become, finally rearing up steeply to form a broken wall of rock around the peaked summit and boulder-strewn top. These rocks display strange and unusual characteristics unlike others found elsewhere; they are not seen from the paths in regular use but merit a leisurely exploration. There is both grace and strength in the uppermost reaches of Bowfell.

Most visitors get their first view of Bowfell from Great Langdale where its dominating presence cannot be ignored: the lower slopes spring sharply from the flat valley pastures and provide an upward route so obvious and inviting that its ascent is almost inevitable. It is a challenge that cannot be denied. Moreover, the way to the summit is simple and straightforward with no problems of route finding, making it eminently suitable as an introduction to fellwalking. Bowfell is a popular climb and a great favourite. Deservedly so. It ranks amongst the best of the Lakeland fells.

(Opposite) Bowfell from Pike o' Blisco

Bowfell from Great Langdale

The walk starts from the car park at the head of Great Langdale with a level half-mile along the access road to Stool End Farm, where the ground immediately beyond rises as a broad grassy buttress between the side valleys of Oxendale, left, and Mickleden, right. This is The Band, a shoulder of Bowfell coming directly down from the summit pyramid and providing the ladder by which the climb is made. The boots of thousands of pilgrims every year have carved a distinct path, with initial variations, from the farm gate. The climb is continuous, without respite, and has little of interest in the vicinity of the path. The Oxendale flank is grassy but the Mickleden slope is craggy, falling away abruptly into shadowy depths occasionally glimpsed from the path. The best features of the rather tedious ascent are the views, as the elevation increases, of the mountains on both sides, Pike o' Blisco standing up grandly across Oxendale and Pike o' Stickle being a most imposing object towering over Mickleden.

(Above) Pike o' Stickle and Loft Crag from The Band; (below) Pike o' Blisco from The Band

When The Band steepens into the final rocky pyramid, the tourist path veers left to the wide depression of Three Tarns, from there reaching the summit by a steep scree path on the right. But to see the best of Bowfell and reach the top by a detour of sustained interest, walkers should keep to the Mickleden edge until a horizontal track turns off along the base of a line of cliffs, Flat Crags. This is the Climbers' Traverse and is a joy to follow. The track runs below the line of cliffs until confronted by a huge rock buttress, Cambridge Crag, which descends to the level of the traverse and, joy of joys, has a spout of clear cold water issuing from a crevice at its base. The situation here is awe-inspiring. Across a scree gully beyond Cambridge Crag rises Bowfell Buttress, a clean-cut tower of rock soaring majestically out of rivers of stones on both sides and affording popular rock-climbing routes: it was to provide easy access to the Buttress that the traverse was devised. Flat Crags and Cambridge Crag appear to be unassailable from this point, and below on the right steep slopes plunge down into the head of Mickleden. Having tasted the waterspout and found it to be nectar, a way of escape from what appears to be a dead end, an impasse, must be sought, and although grandmothers and infants may consider it prudent to turn back here, for active walkers there is hope of further progress upwards by a scramble up the pile of boulders and stones on the left side of Cambridge Crag, a hope soon to be fulfilled.

(Below) The Climbers' Traverse   *(Opposite) Bowfell Buttress from the foot of Cambridge Crag*

In the course of the scramble up the edge of Cambridge Crag, an extraordinary scene unfolds: stretching away to the left is a vast slab of rock, naked except where vegetation has gained a roothold in the cracks and crevices. It is really the upper part of Flat Crags, tilted at an angle so easy that it can be walked upon. The top rim is seen to take the form of a low parapet, like a giant kerbstone. This unusual feature is unique and has no counterpart elsewhere in the district. I call it the Great Slab.

The Great Slab

The summit of Bowfell looking to the Scafell range

Easier ground is reached at the top of Cambridge Crag, but easier only in the sense that the gradient is less steep. It has, however, a covering of boulders and care should be exercised in crossing them towards the summit, which is now in view ahead.

I was once gingerly picking my way through these boulders when one heeled over and trapped my leg against another. Happily I was able to heave it back into its original socket and went on my way, only realising later that I might have been securely held and unable to free myself. This incident happened within shouting distance of the tourist path and no doubt I would have been rescued later in the day. But what an ignominy that would have been for an advocate of solitary fellwalking!

Before going up to the summit cairn, a detour half-left, crossing the well-trodden popular path, leads to the edge overlooking the Three Tarns depression and another of Bowfell's unusual formations is revealed. From the edge a dozen short scree gullies fall away steeply, one after another and all to a pattern, as though seamed by a giant comb. These are the Links of Bowfell.

Here ends an hour's exciting exploration of Bowfell's secret nooks and crannies and rock scenery, all unseen and unsuspected by walkers who adhere rigidly to the popular route of ascent. Now for the ultimate reward: the summit at 2960 ft.

A large cairn surmounts a chaotic upheaval of boulders in a surround of rocky outcrops and stones: here is nature in the raw. It is likely that the top will be populated by other walkers; if so it is to be hoped that they are quietly enjoying their achievement and not being too noisily exultant about it. I like to have mountain summits all to myself. They are the loneliest of places and are best appreciated in silence. Human discords, loud conversations, shouting, raucous laughter and the modern evil of transistor radios are totally out of place. If such distractions occur on Bowfell's summit they must be endured, for the all-round view should not be hurriedly dismissed but studied at all points of the compass; this is a panorama that many consider to be the finest in Lakeland.

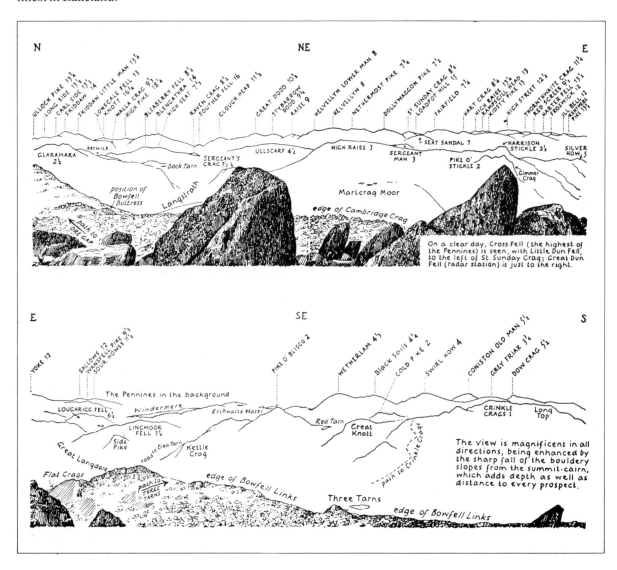

The neighbouring fell of Esk Pike is the next objective, and the path going up to its summit from the intermediate depression of Ore Gap can be seen from afar. Ore Gap is reached by a path along the top of Bowfell's north ridge, where a deviation to the right gives a downward view of the topmost rocks of Bowfell Buttress and, further, the crags of Hanging Knotts. The path is well cairned, now unnecessarily so because boots have scoured a blazed track that can be followed easily even in bad conditions. This over-abundance of cairns occurs on many mountain paths. Originally, when the paths were sketchy and intermittent, these piles of stones were useful in guiding walkers along the right tracks, especially in mist, but such is the recent popularity of fellwalking that most paths have become distinct and can be followed without the help of cairns, but they are still a reassuring comfort when visibility is restricted to a few yards.

Ore Gap, a narrow col, is also variously known as Ure Gap and Ewer Gap, but Ore is probably the correct spelling of the name and is certainly appropriate, for a pronounced vein of hematite passes through the depression, the evidence being plain to see in the red soil exposed along the path.

If it is desired to shorten the walk a quick descent can be made from Ore Gap to Angle Tarn and the Langdale path down on the right, but those more resolute will cross the gap and continue up the obvious path leading to the top of Esk Pike.

Esk Pike is a rare example of a fell given its name by walkers. It was nameless on maps until quite recently but was increasingly referred to as Esk Pike, appropriately because it stands at the head of Eskdale, and this name has now been adopted by the Ordnance Survey. The summit is notable for its colourful rocks which, unlike those on the other tops in this area of Borrowdale volcanics, are sharp and splintery, of natural hues of brown and white and splashed with green lichens. The highest point is a craggy outcrop, rising out of a debris of flaked and fragmented stones. In the lee of the summit crag, which is cut away vertically on the north side, is a shelter formed by substantial walls, a good refuge in storms and quite the most effective of all mountain shelters.

The walk continues in the same direction and a descent is made to the wide grassy depression of Esk Hause, with the massive bulk of Great End beyond and a view down to the left into the wild recesses of upper Eskdale.

Esk Hause

Esk Hause is the furthest point of the walk. The easy slope on the right is next descended to a very familiar landmark: a large wall shelter on the highest part of the popular pedestrian highway that links Great Langdale and Wasdale and is commonly but incorrectly referred to as Esk Hause. The true Esk Hause was left five minutes ago. Early photographs show a wooden signpost here, but this like many others has gone, probably to fuel camp fires.

The wall shelter on the Great Langdale – Wasdale path

The Langdale path is followed to the right down a long easy slope, with Langstrath opening up on the left, and arrives alongside Angle Tarn, a dark and sinister sheet of water in the shadow of the crags of Hanging Knotts but a welcome and refreshing halting place often frequented by naked bathers. Issuing from it, and crossed by the path, is Angletarn Gill, a feeder of Langstrath Beck.

Angle Tarn

Beyond Angle Tarn there is a short rise to Rossett Pass, the path then declining to the top of Rossett Gill, probably the best known and certainly the least liked and most abused walkers' route in the district. Thousands upon thousands of booted pedestrians every year have scraped away all vestiges of greenery and transformed a once-quiet watercourse into a wide channel of loose scree, toilsome to ascend and unpleasant to descend. Nobody has a good word to say about Rossett Gill. For years I toiled up and down this dusty ladder of stones without being aware of an alternative route, but a happy purchase of a set of the 1901 edition of the Ordnance Survey maps on the scale of six inches to a mile, and a study thereof, disclosed the existence of a pony route that had obviously fallen into disuse and been omitted from later maps; it was a route that avoided the gill completely and followed a circuitous course along the lower slopes of Bowfell. I went along to trace it and had little difficulty in doing so: it was intermittent in places but was gently graded and skilfully constructed to ease the passage of laden ponies. It was a pleasure to walk upon. Never again would I suffer the scourge of Rossett Gill.

I was able to obtain some information about this ancient track from a native of Langdale who had a knowledge of earlier days in the valley. It is believed that it had been used for the secret transport of goods smuggled into Ravenglass and carried over the hills by packhorses. My informant also told me of a packwoman's grave near the gill, out of the sight of passing walkers, and from his precise instructions I was able to locate it, finding it to be marked by stones laid on the ground in the form of a cross; the exact situation I have never disclosed to avoid disturbance. This is the grave of a woman who regularly called at Langdale farms carrying a pack of articles for sale and whose mortal remains were found and buried here 190 years ago. Another feature of the pony route is a hidden sheepfold, cleverly screened from the valley below and used by the dalesmen to conceal their sheep in the far-off days of border raids. Beyond the sheepfold, the path serves as a causeway to a small natural pool, and then turns down to Mickleden, still far below.

In the later stages of the pony route, a few ancient cairns act as guides down the grassy slopes of Green Tongue. This final section is not distinct underfoot (although, as is often the case, clearly discernible from a distance) but the descent on grass to the floor of the valley is simple. The point of the crossing of Mickleden Beck by the packhorses is obscure but the stream can conveniently be forded at several places to join the well-trodden path along Mickleden leading to Dungeon Ghyll and the car park. Few, having done this walk, will drive away without a long last look at Bowfell: a look not only of respect but probably even of affection born of their close and intimate acquaintance with this grand mountain.

Rossett Gill

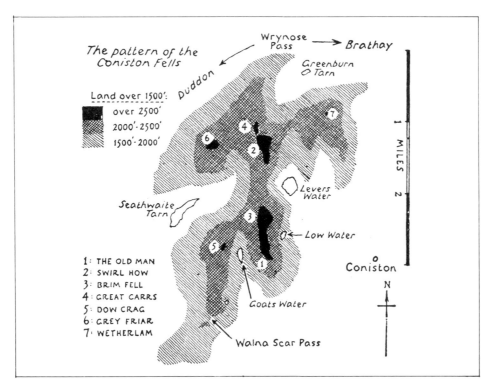

The pattern of the Coniston Fells

Land over 1500':
- over 2500'
- 2000'-2500'
- 1500'-2000'

Wrynose Pass → Brathay

Duddon

Greenburn Tarn

Seathwaite Tarn

Levers Water

Low Water

Coniston

1: THE OLD MAN
2: SWIRL HOW
3: BRIM FELL
4: GREAT CARRS
5: DOW CRAG
6: GREY FRIAR
7: WETHERLAM

Goats Water

Walna Scar Pass

N

1 MILES 2

The Coniston Fells are a separate geographical unit, almost entirely severed from the adjacent mountain areas of Lakeland by the Duddon and Brathay valleys which form clearly defined boundaries to the group, the only high link with neighbouring fells occurring at the watershed between the two river systems, Wrynose Pass. Until 1974, these natural boundaries were adopted for local government purposes, the Coniston Fells being wholly within the county of Lancashire; an anachronism, really, because in appearance and character and traditions they are an integral part of the Lake District, as much so as Cumberland and Westmorland which shared the other fell country in the region. In 1974, the Rivers Duddon and Brathay lost administrative significance, the Furness area of Lancashire including the Coniston Fells being merged with Cumberland and Westmorland in the new county of Cumbria, a reorganisation justified by geographical considerations. Lancashire thus lost its finest scenery, a favoured and favourite territory that the people of that county had been proud to claim as their own.

The high ground of the Coniston group takes the form of a semi-circle, with two major off-shoots, and comprises several named fells with distinctive summits. Of these, Coniston Old Man is the most popular objective of sojourners in the village of Coniston, its ascent being almost a ritual undertaken by visitors of all ages, from babies in rucksacks to senior citizens supported by sticks, all toiling upwards in a staggered and staggering procession. The Old Man is regarded as a shrine, and many are its pilgrims.

(Opposite) Coniston Old Man from Lad Stones

No mountain in Lakeland has been more cruelly exploited than Coniston Old Man. His breast is pierced by a labyrinth of the tunnels and shafts of abandoned copper mines, and great slices have been, and are being, cut away to produce a green slate internationally in demand for its beautiful colour, fine texture and durability. The eastern flank is an industrial mess of old workings and dusty access roads. Yet the Old Man remains a benevolent giant revered by generations of walkers and is held in high esteem by the inhabitants of the village he shelters, for he has contributed much to their prosperity. Despite all his ugly scars, the Old Man retains a proud and dignified bearing, shedding his tears quietly into a lovely tarn at the base of the summit escarpment. He has seen better days but, despite his mutilations, more people than ever come to pay their respects.

It is a common practice of active walkers after arriving at the summit of the Old Man to continue north over Brim Fell to Swirl How, there crossing to Wetherlam and returning to Coniston by the ridge of Lad Stones. This is a splendid high-level walk, usually referred to as the 'Coniston Round', nowhere difficult and on terrain that is kind to the feet. But it omits the grandest feature of the Coniston Fells, this highlight being the tremendous rock-face of Dow Crag, one of the greatest scenes in the district and for the past hundred years a Mecca for rock climbers. Dow Crag is too good to be left out of a walk on the Coniston Fells and can conveniently be included in the itinerary of the usual Coniston Round, having as a further advantage a quiet approach that avoids quarrying activity and the busy tourist path.

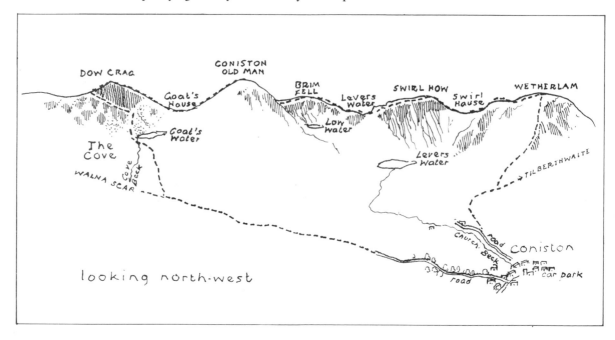

The approach to Dow Crag

Leave Coniston by the steep tarmac road leading up past the former railway station for three-quarters of a mile to the open fell and the Walna Scar path. Here at the end of the tarmac, a quarry road turns off to the right and there is parking space for cars. There is nothing to be gained by leaving a car here on this occasion, however, the return not being made to this point but directly to the village.

The Walna Scar path is followed along the base of the Old Man, the first section having been widened and roughly surfaced to serve a quarry, after which it continues distinctly and climbs gradually. The desolate moor declining on the left has a considerable antiquarian interest, having revealed evidences that it was the home of a Bronze Age population; in modern times, it achieved a fleeting national publicity when a young walker sighted a flying saucer close overhead and produced a convincing photograph to support his story. In the absence of any such distractions, the walk continues through a natural rock gateway and soon afterwards a cairned track branches to the right; this is followed into a mountain amphitheatre known as The Cove, where Dow Crag is revealed ahead.

The first glimpse of the crag is impressive and becomes more so with every step along the track, which leads eager walkers to the outlet of a large tarn, Goat's Water, deeply inurned in a wild setting with Dow Crag high above. Amongst the rocks of the issuing stream there was formerly a simple memorial stone inscribed 'Charmer 1911', Charmer being a foxhound killed in a fall from the crag. Charmer rests in peace but not so his memorial, which unkind hands have uprooted and cast aside: it is now difficult to find amongst the boulders of the stream bed. Poor Charmer: in life he was greatly loved, surely in death he deserved more respect?

Charmer's Grave

The outlet of Goat's Water is forded and a track rising across slopes of scree is followed to a pile of large boulders forming a cave below the lowest part of the crag, which now looks fearfully imposing and even intimidating as it soars above. The cliffs are palpably unassailable except by supermen; knees tremble at the thought of venturing upwards. However, by proceeding along the base of the buttresses on the left on a rising course and passing the gloomy cleft of Great Gully, a stony recess is reached where Easy Gully (so called) debouches in a chaotic welter of stones and boulders. Easy Gully offers a direct ascent to the ridge above for rock-climbers only, but for lesser mortals there is a line of escape to the left, where a stony rake, steep but crag-free, leads up to easier ground above: this I call South Rake. At the top, now again on welcome grass, a turn to the right and a final short scramble on rocks brings the summit of Dow Crag underfoot.

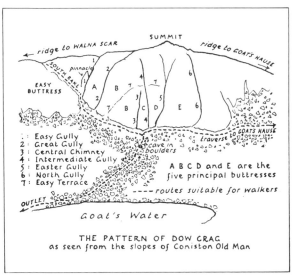

(Opposite) Dow Crag across Goat's Water; (below left) Looking down Dow Crag; (below right) Dow Crag from the path to the Old Man

(Left) The summit of Dow Crag; (right) Goat's Water from Goat's Hause

Dow Crag, 2555 ft, has one of the most delectable summits in the whole of Lakeland, taking the form of a small neat peak of piled rocks, an exquisite perch elevated above a frightful precipice and having a sensational view of Goat's Water nearly a thousand feet below. To attain it, even after cheating by using the easy South Rake, gives a satisfaction little less than would have been felt after a direct climb up the crag. This is the grandest spot on the walk and should be savoured to the full before departing.

Next there is a long and easy descent along the rim of the crags to Goat's Hause, a col linking Dow Crag with Coniston Old Man and having a full length view of Goat's Water, and then a steady climb inclining right to the top of the Old Man on ground broken by small outcrops of slate in unusual formations of vertical flakes. Human noise often indicates the position of the summit cairn before it can be seen.

There is a wide prospect of the Furness district and the waters of Morecambe Bay from the summit of the Old Man, and a strongly-built platform of slate on the highest point is, almost as a traditional custom, often occupied by parties of visitors obsessed in a search for Blackpool Tower on the far horizon. There has been some wavering by the Ordnance Survey about the height of the mountain, 2631 ft, 2633 ft and 2635 ft being variously quoted on their maps before resolving the doubt by switching to the new-fangled metres, a change deplored by all who take a pride in the hills. Now the Old Man has been demoted from 2631 ft or 2633 ft or 2635 ft to 803m which, after all he has suffered, is surely a case of adding insult to injury.

The next objective is the large cairn on Brim Fell, reached by a simple stroll along the edge of the cliffs plunging down on the right to Low Water. There is little cause for delay here and a long descent follows to the depression of Levers Hause, named after the large tarn of Levers Water seen down on the right; a dam constructed at its outflow ensured ample supplies of water for the copper mines.

(Above) The summit of Coniston Old Man; (below) Levers Water from Levers Hause

(Opposite) Brim Fell from Little How Crags   *(Above) Great Carrs from the summit of Swirl How*

Beyond Levers Hause, there is a steady climb to come alongside the upper fringe of Little How Crags and Great How Crags and then the gradient eases, levelling out to give a simple approach to the cairn on Swirl How, 2630 ft, which is found to stand on the verge of a profound abyss to the north, where the Greenburn valley lies far below a downfall of crags and scree.

Swirl How is the hub of the Coniston Fells, having an altitude only inches lower than that of the Old Man, and being the pivot of three important ridges. The views, too, are more embracing; of the nearer surroundings, Great Carrs most catches the eye, its east face an unbroken tumble of crags and screes into Greenburn. Great Carrs was the scene of a wartime aeroplane crash, its top still having parts of the undercarriage scattered around and the wrecked fuselage visible in a gully below.

The summit of Swirl How is very pleasant on the right sort of day, a place to linger and enjoy a wonderful panorama. It is, moreover, relatively unfrequented, quiet and uncluttered by babies and senior citizens, a place for undisturbed meditation and appreciation of the gift of legs and these friendly fells on which to exercise them, a place to count blessings.

Prison Band from the lower slopes of Black Sails

The walk now turns east, sharply descending the rocky ridge of Prison Band and so reaching Swirl Hause, a pass between the Greenburn valley on the left and Coniston via Levers Water on the right. Beyond the hause, a further climb leads to the subsidiary top of Black Sails and forward to the stony summit of Wetherlam and a fine prospect over Little Langdale and Windermere to the distant Pennines.

The summit of Wetherlam

Wetherlam, like the Old Man, has an eastern flank pock-marked with the relics of disused workings and the shafts and tunnels of old mines. In lengthy explorations here I have counted a hundred man-made openings in the ground, many of them without protection and very dangerous. Wander not on Wetherlam after dark!

All that remains to be done to complete the walk is to proceed along the declining south ridge of Wetherlam (no path and no difficulties). Lower down, the ridge is known as Lad Stones, and here by veering down the slope on the left a good path coming from Tilberthwaite is joined; this descends to a road in Coppermines Valley that goes down alongside Church Beck and an attractive waterfall to enter the main street of Coniston.

Waterfall, Church Beck

11 THE NEWLANDS ROUND
FROM LITTLE TOWN   (9 MILES)

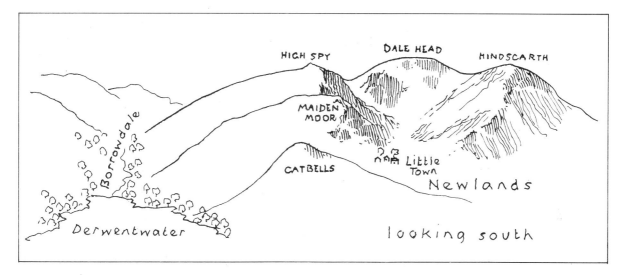

More than fifty years have gone by since I first set eyes on Newlands and in all that time the valley seems not to have changed in any way. Today it is the same sweet Arcadia I knew so long ago, lovely and secluded, an idyllic place of flowers and trees, of emerald pastures and sequestered farmsteads, all cosily sheltered by rough mountains, and having as its greatest blessing an undisturbed peace, a freedom from tourists in the mass and related commercial enterprises, and enjoying a way of life that in essence has never altered.

The Newlands valley runs closely parallel to Borrowdale yet is a world apart. Borrowdale at all seasons of the year and especially in summer is heavily populated by visitors attracted by Derwentwater and the exquisite scenery of the lake's environs, but the charms of Newlands are subtle and appeal more to a discerning minority. A lofty range of hills between the two is an effective barrier, segregating one from the other and allowing each to live its life without dependence on its neighbour.

The range of hills springs from the western shore of Derwentwater, rising first to the shapely cone of Catbells and continuing at an increasing elevation over Maiden Moor and the summit of High Spy, with Borrowdale now far below the eastern flank and Newlands a deep and narrowing trench at the foot of the precipitous western slopes. The high ground then swings round to its focal point, the massive bulk of Dale Head which, as its name implies, terminates the valley, and next turns north along the Hindscarth ridge, thus confining the upper reaches between steep acclivities. It is this 'horseshoe' that provides the walk to be described: a circuit of the skyline around the wild recesses of Newlands beyond the limits of cultivation.

(Opposite) The upper reaches of Newlands

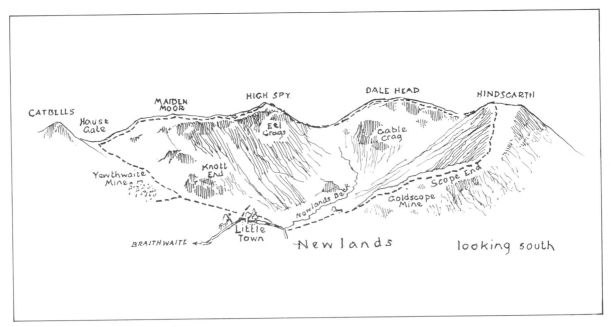

CATBELLS · House Gate · MAIDEN MOOR · HIGH SPY · Eel Crags · DALE HEAD · Cable Crag · HINDSCARTH · Knott End · Yewthwaite Mine · Scope End · Goldscope Mine · Newlands Beck · BRAITHWAITE · Little Town · Newlands · looking south

Knott End from Newlands Church

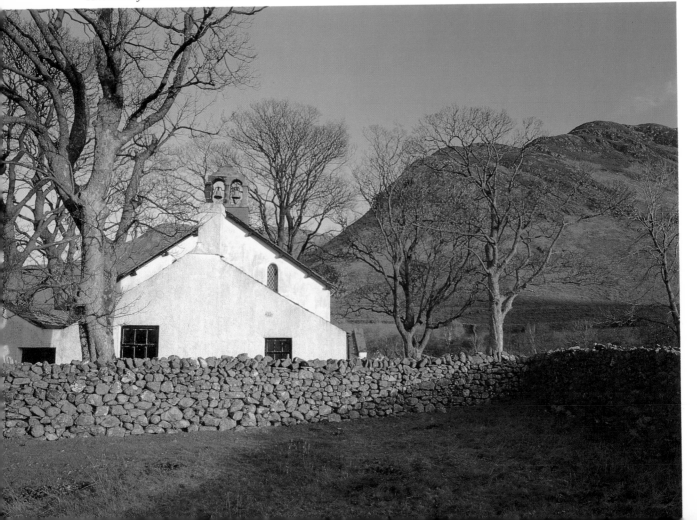

I prefer to begin and end the walk at the hamlet of Little Town, where a path joins a rising cart-track on the open fell below the crags of Knott End; at a wall-corner, the cart-track turns left and a path going straight ahead is followed, passing an area despoiled by the disused Yewthwaite Mine where there are dangerous open shafts, a tragic death occurring in one of them in 1962. Directly ahead is the depression of Hause Gate and upon reaching it a glorious view of Derwentwater and Borrowdale is suddenly revealed. Cameras should not be clicked here, however, as an even better viewpoint will soon be reached.

From Hause Gate a track to the right mounts steadily to Maiden Moor, aiming for a prominent cairn that appears to be the summit, but isn't. This cairn is a viewpoint par excellence: it commands an out-of-this-world prospect of Derwentwater backed by Blencathra, a scene that nobody carrying a camera can possibly resist.

Derwentwater from Maiden Moor

Dale Head from High Spy

The top of Maiden Moor is an easy promenade over level ground with little of immediate interest, and although the Ordnance Survey state the height as 1887 ft there is doubt as to the precise spot that yielded this information. All is grass here: there is no stone to sit on nor an outcrop to recline against, and the best features of the retrospective view are now hidden by widening convex slopes, so that there is no cause to linger. Walkers who feel they have earned a halt are recommended to stroll across to the Newlands edge of the summit plateau and find a couch near the rim of the formidable Bull Crag and enjoy a bird's view of the valley; it will be noted that Bull Crag is a part only of a continuous escarpment along this side of the fell. It is, in fact, more exciting to continue the walk along the edge of the escarpment than it is to keep to the popular path. Further on, the moor narrows to a crest and then an engineered path climbs to the summit cairn on High Spy, 2143 ft, a fine vantage point immediately above the mile-long precipice of Eel Crags, down which, from safe stances, there are spectacular views of the head of Newlands. But the most imposing object in sight, its full stature now revealed, is Dale Head, its steep northern face, wrinkled by tiers of crags, effectively bringing the valley to an abrupt end.

Next follows the first descent of the day, a long downhill walk to the moorland east of Dale Head, a confusing terrain of hillocks and hollows; here the valley path comes up out of Newlands and can be used for a quick return to Little Town in case of an onset of bad weather or to save time or tired legs. Other paths go down to Borrowdale, left, and forward to Honister Pass. The place to aim for is Dalehead Tarn, indicated from afar by its shimmering waters, and here, looking back, the profile of Eel Crags can be seen taking shape below the summit of High Spy.

Dalehead Tarn and High Spy

From the far end of Dalehead Tarn the ascent to the summit of Dale Head starts, there being a track for most of the way. This climb is steep and, like all climbs, longer than expected. I well remember, in the days when I was a raw apprentice on the hills, ill-prepared and ill-equipped, toiling up this slope in a state of near exhaustion: there was no track then and the ascent seemed interminable; for the last few hundred yards I was reduced to crawling upwards on hands and knees. As always on the hills, a five-minute halt was enough to restore sufficient energy to enable me to go on my way. In those far-off days, too, my routine was to descend steep grass by shuffling down on my bottom, a practice I still adopt on occasion because a tough and rubbery bottom is a valuable agent of friction, a sheet anchor with superb resistance to the pull of gravity. Once this method of downward progression ended in calamity when a concealed rock neatly removed the seat of my pants, a matter of indifference while I was alone on the hills but in the streets of Keswick later, and on the bus going home, I had to hide my embarrassed flesh in a buttoned-up plastic raincoat although the day was sunny and warm and everybody else was in shirt sleeves. Since then, my advice to others is to keep the body erect when walking steeply up or down.

Summit cairn, Dale Head

The toil of the ascent is immediately forgotten on arrival at the summit of Dale Head. In every direction the panorama is magnificent, especially excelling in the full-length view of Newlands, the wild upper valley merging into the sylvan scenery beyond and distant Skiddaw closing the picture perfectly. This I consider to be the finest aerial view of a valley from a Lakeland summit. The well-constructed cairn of neat courses of slate stands on the brink of a sharp drop and makes a striking foreground. I have had reports that this cairn has suffered wanton damage of late but hope they are not true. I have an affection for summit cairns. To me, they represent ambitions and achievements. I feel bereaved by their loss.

Dale Head is a mountain mutilated by prospectors. The Honister flank is pitted with quarries and the Newlands face bears traces of a disused copper mine where the bright green veins of copper malachite can still be seen in the rocks and stones. It is a mountain of interest to geologists, for beneath the carpet of grass there is a fusion of the Skiddaw slates and the volcanic rocks of central Lakeland, some evidences of this joint being seen on the actual summit.

(Below) Eel Crags and High Spy from Dale Head; (opposite) The Newlands valley from Dale Head

Dale Head is the turning point of the walk. A narrowing ridge, scarped on both sides and having lovely views of the Buttermere valley and fells, is traversed north-west to a depression where the ridge is left and a plateau crossed due north for half a mile to the summit of Hindscarth, 2385 ft, a fell with a broad top but extremely steep flanks on both sides. The summit cairn is an untidy pile of stones amongst embedded rocks; of greater interest is a larger and well-built cairn of some antiquity 200 paces away with the interior hollowed to act as a wind-shelter. There is now a long descent north, with cliffs falling away on the right, to the narrow ridge of Scope End directly ahead, where a delightful track through heather winds down towards the valley.

The upper part of the Newlands valley is rich in minerals and there are many places where man has scratched the ground for buried treasure, mainly lead and copper, and on Scope End, gold. Here was the famous Goldscope Mine, about which I wrote in an earlier publication as follows:

Goldscope Mine

Goldscope Mine was abandoned a hundred years ago after intermittent operation over a period of six centuries. One of the oldest mines in the district, it was also the most important in output, having rich veins of lead and copper. Silver and gold, too, have been extracted. Its early development, on a large scale, was undertaken by Germans, and its long history has been marked by many adventures and much litigation.

Upper Pan Holes

External evidence of the mine is indicated mainly by spoil-heaps on the Newlands Beck side of Scope End: immediately above is the main adit of Lower Pan Holes (from which a stream issues) with a second opening a few yards higher, under a tree. Further up the fellside is a curious slanting gash in a rockface — the Upper Pan Holes. On the other (Scope Beck) flank of the ridge are several levels.

Scope End is therefore pierced from both sides and the main level runs into the fell for such a considerable distance (over 300 yards) before becoming impassable, due to roof-falls, that it is reasonable to suppose that in the later years of operation it would be possible to walk right through the heart of it. In the darkness of these inner workings is a great shaft, which was sunk to such a depth ultimately that the pumping of water from it became too costly — this, not exhaustion of the minerals, was the reason for closure.

Lower Pan Holes

Hindscarth and Scope End

Having survived an exploration of the Goldscope Mine, the descent of Scope End is continued to the farm of Low Snab at its foot, where the farm access road goes through fields to Newlands Church, a small and humble edifice plain or pretty according to the eyes of the beholder and thence to the main valley road, reached at a bridge over Newlands Beck. Little Town is up a short hill to the right where, looking back, there is a splendid view of Hindscarth and Scope End, fitting subjects for the last photograph of the day.

12 THE COLEDALE ROUND
FROM BRAITHWAITE   (9 MILES)

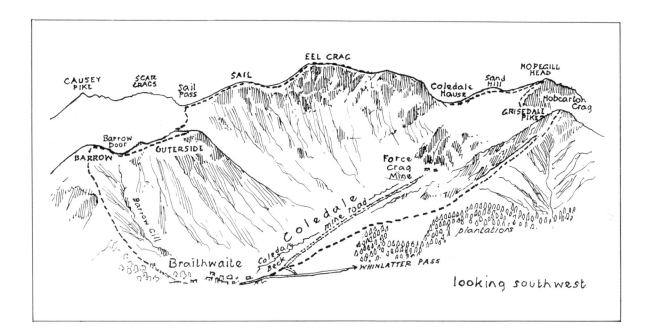

Nobody ever goes into raptures about Coledale. It lacks the characteristics of other Lakeland valleys, being without a farmstead, trees and green pastures and having no sylvan corners, no sinuous curves and no lovely paths. There is nothing to explore: all is seen at a glance and is not inviting. It is a long straight trench along which runs a rough road to the Force Crag barytes mine at its distant head, where the valley terminates in a spectacular tumble of cliffs and waterfalls: the end is dramatic, the approach dull and tedious. Coledale is not a place for a picnic.

The valley has one great advantage for the walker. Although a long and uninspiring trudge, the mine road offers a fast passage to the heart of a group of fells of considerable merit. And it is tightly enclosed by a ring of rugged heights that can be linked at a high level on a continuous walk all round the valley, a walk that ranks amongst the best in sustained interest and in the excellence of the views from each of the six summits attained.

The valley of Coledale is without charm but will be remembered with affection by those who walk around the mountain skyline of its perimeter and by so doing enjoy one of their most rewarding days on the tops.

(Opposite) The head of Coledale

On the principle of getting the hardest part of the climbing done first to give tired limbs an easy return to base, a policy I strongly advocate, I suggest that the walk starts from Braithwaite with an ascent of the mountain that dominates the village, Grisedale Pike. The climbing commences at once. Every step beyond the last cottage is upwards until the summit is reached, a long and relentless fight against gravity for which a girding of the loins is an essential preliminary.

Grisedale Pike from Braithwaite

Where the road turns right for Whinlatter, eager walkers have blazed a steep track straight up the fellside, but it is easier to go up the road a short way and use the mine road which turns left at a gravel pit to reach the walkers' path at a higher level. Now the climbing starts in earnest with a steep pull up to the 1200 ft contour. Here there is relief from intense effort as the gradient eases to the final pyramid of the Pike, the last section entailing more collar-work for half an hour until the summit is reached at 2593 ft, the cairn standing on a plinth of slate amidst a litter of fragments that tinkle musically when walked upon. A halt here is deserved and may be spent enjoying a wide prospect of the coastal plain and the Solway Firth, but most attention will be focussed on the next stages of the walk, well displayed between south and west.

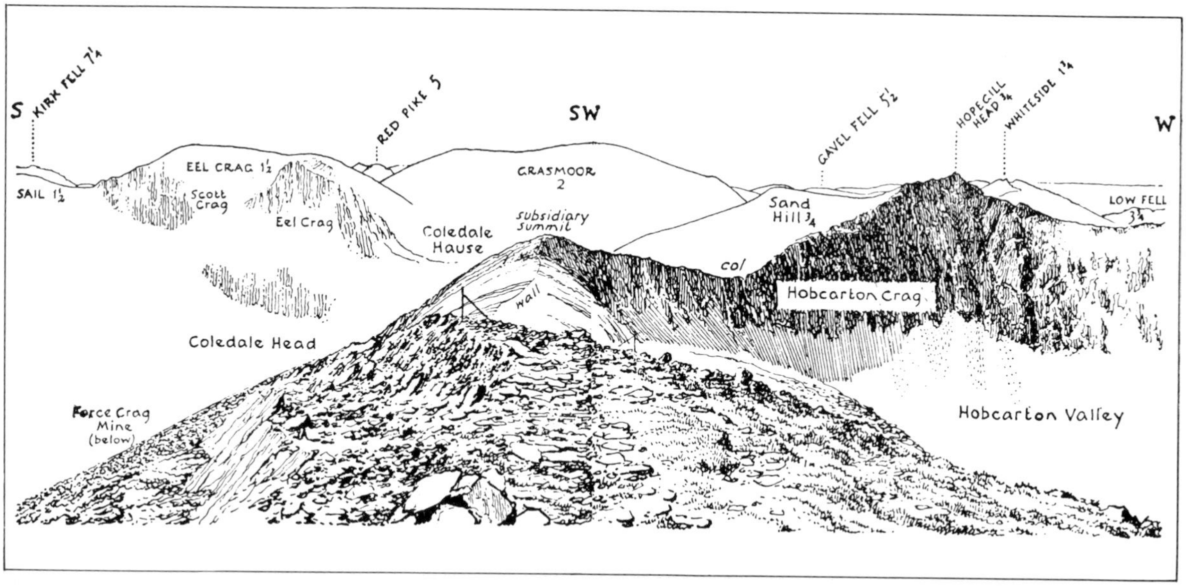
S
KIRK FELL 7¼
RED PIKE 5
SW
GAVEL FELL 5½
HOPEGILL HEAD ¾
WHITESIDE 1¼
W
SAIL 1½
EEL CRAG 1½
Scott Crag
Eel Crag
GRASMOOR 2
Coledale Hause
subsidiary summit
Sand Hill ¾
LOW FELL 3¾
col
wall
Hobcarton Crag
Coledale Head
Force Crag Mine (below)
Hobcarton Valley

Keswick and Derwentwater from the summit of Grisedale Pike

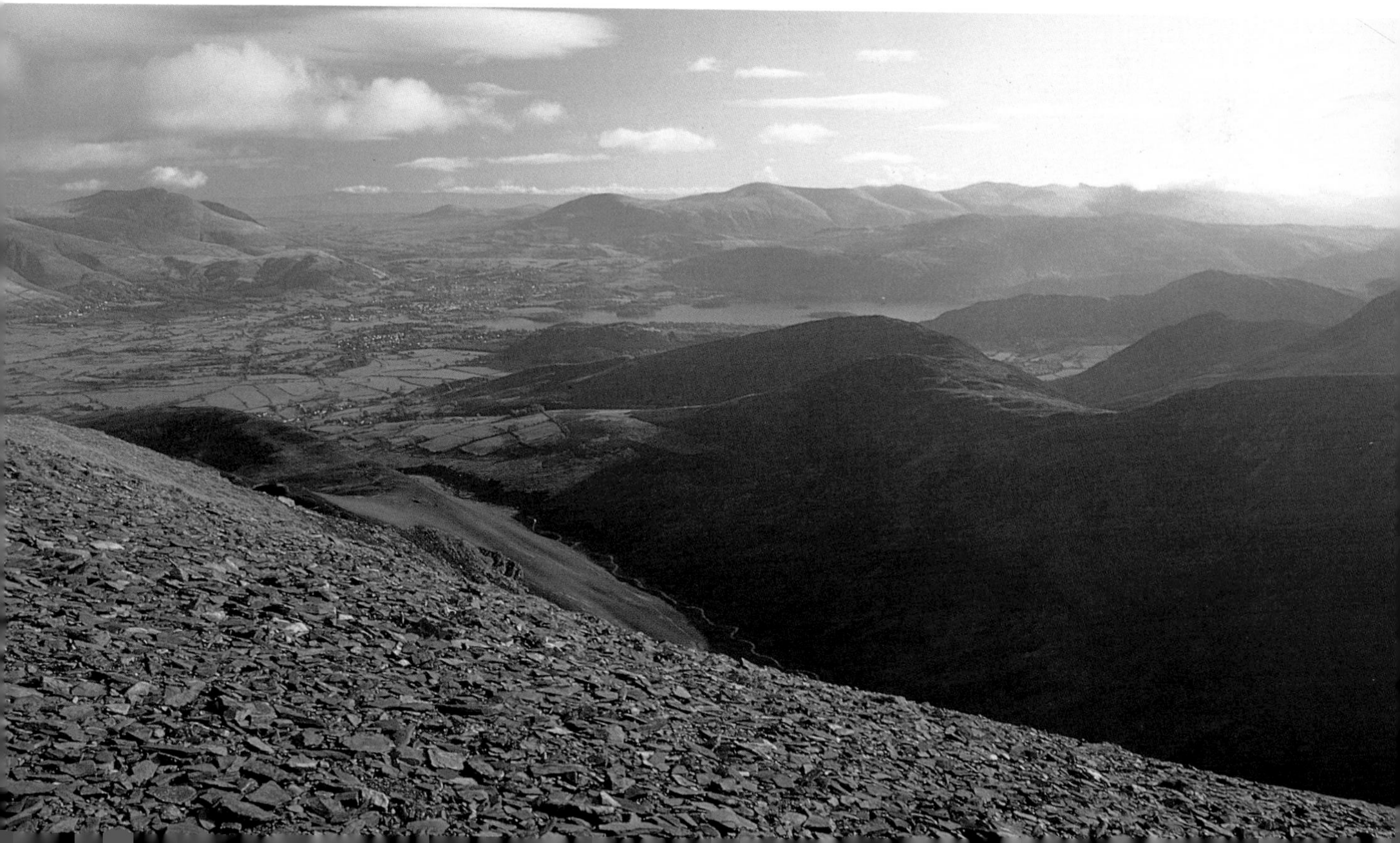

Hobcarton Crag appears ahead as an increasingly formidable object as the walk is resumed down an easy ridge to a slight depression, beyond which a gradual climb along the edge of the cliffs reaches the peaked summit of Hopegill Head, 2525 ft, a wonderful vantage point immediately above a wild downfall of crags interspersed with lush terraces of bilberry. This is a hallowed place for botanists, being the only known habitat in England of the red alpine catchfly (*Viscaria alpina*), but searches for this rare plant are most certainly not recommended: the near-vertical rocks are of Skiddaw slate, fractured and splintered and totally unsafe for exploration. It is significant that no rock-climbing takes place here.

Viscaria alpina

Hobcarton Crag

Eel Crag above Coledale House

On one occasion I had a remarkable experience on the top of Hopegill Head. I approached the summit by way of the rocky northern ridge and, while yet some distance away, became aware of a great commotion at the cairn. I could hear a symphony of twittering and the swish of wings, growing in volume as I drew nearer, and as I topped the last rocks and brought the cairn in sight the cause was revealed: some thirty or forty swifts were darting and diving around the cairn, obviously in a state of great excitement because they completely ignored my presence only a few yards away; they had other things to engage their attention. They swooped around my head with alarming insistence, coming within inches before wheeling away; the experience was rather frightening, like something from a nightmare or a horror film. This was the only time I came within five yards of a summit cairn yet was unable to reach it: that short distance was made untenable by the diving swifts, but I was near enough to see that the pile of stones was covered by flying ants and that I was disturbing a feast. On other occasions I have found colonies of winged ants on summit cairns but unattended by predators, and once on the top of Caw in the Duddon Valley I found the cairn completely plastered with ladybirds, the stones appearing to be stained a bright red. These migrating flights of insects seem to have a liking for coming to rest at summit cairns, bless their little hearts, just as I have.

The rocky top of Hopegill Head is the finest situation visited on the walk and is left with reluctance to pass over the subsidiary height of Sand Hill and descend a grass slope to the wide depression of Coledale Hause, which carries a path coming up out of Coledale across a watershed and down to Lanthwaite by way of Gasgale Gill. The only feature of interest here is an old water cut made to divert supplies from Gasgale Gill for use at the Force Crag Mine in Coledale. Across the hause are the stony slopes of Eel Crag, the next objective.

Eel Crag has two summits, a lower one at 2649 ft reached by an unpleasant scramble over loose stones from Coledale Hause (which can be avoided by going up alongside Gasgale Gill until strips of grass appear on the left) and the main one at 2749 ft, the latter having a triangulation column. The name by which the fell is commonly known, Eel Crag, is unfortunate and inaccurate, the name properly being that of a rock buttress overlooking Coledale. The Ordnance Survey give the name of the fell as Crag Hill, but I never heard anyone use this. It is the hub of a mountain group, with four ridges radiating from it. The Coledale face drops away sharply and is much broken by crags; even steeper is the southern flank falling to Sail Beck, a pathless wilderness of eroded cliffs and scree and heather where no man ventures.

(Above) Sail Beck and Knott Rigg from Sail   *(Opposite) Coledale Head from Sail Pass*

Beyond the main cairn of Eel Crag, a ridge leaves the summit and goes sharply down eastwards, becoming narrow and rocky but without difficulty and is followed by a short rise to the summit of Sail, 2530 ft and then a long descent to Sail Pass which is crossed by a little-used path linking Stoneycroft in Newlands and Buttermere.

Beyond Sail Pass, the ridge continues over Scar Crags and ends abruptly at Causey Pike, but these heights are outside the ambit of Coledale, and at Sail Pass the path descending left below Long Comb is taken, soon arriving at the site of Lakeland's only cobalt mine, long abandoned. Continuing, now on the old mine road, there is a crossing of easy ground in the wide expanse of High Moss. This old road becomes of cart width and leads directly down to Stoneycroft in Newlands, two tarmac miles from Braithwaite, and offers a quick return to base. But walkers with a reserve of energy should climb the slope of Outerside, rising to the left of High Moss, and so reach its summit at 1863 ft. Here there is an aerial view of Coledale and a comprehensive prospect of the whole walk so far done and still to be done. Otherwise the top is undistinguished.

Grisedale Pike from Outerside

Outerside is rarely visited but a thin track through the heather heading north-east and having the Coledale edge on the left goes pleasantly down to the depression of Low Moss and then bypasses the minor height of Stile End, curving round it to the pronounced gap of Barrow Door. A path going down to Braithwaite passes through this gap, and if followed to the left gives a quick return to the village alongside the surprising ravine of Barrow Gill. But there is another summit to be visited to complete the itinerary: at 1494 ft this is the lowest top of the day but, thanks to a carpet of heather, a delightful belvedere. This is Barrow, easily reached by a rising track from Barrow Door and much too good to be missed.

(Above) Barrow Door

View from the summit of Barrow

From the summit of Barrow a bewitching path descends its northern ridge, at first winding through heather and lower down on grass amidst bracken, the sort of path that tempts one to linger even though ravaged by hunger and knowing a good meal awaits ahead. There is an exquisite vista of Newlands down to the right, marred at one point where the debris of the old Barrow Mine falls from the ridge and scars the fellside.

The end of this delectable path is reached at the farm of Braithwaite Lodge, where an access road goes down to the village. Now for that meal!

13 SCAFELL PIKE
FROM BORROWDALE   (10 MILES)

Ridges, in general, provide the best fellwalking in Lakeland as elsewhere: they are the high-level traverses that link mountain summits without too much descent and re-ascent between them. Ridges are usually the easiest lines of progression in rough terrain; they are the natural passages along the tops, and invariably reward the walker with ever-changing distant panoramas and aerial views of ethereal beauty as lakes and bright fields edged with trees and copses come into sight far below; and, in sharp contrast, tarns nestling in dark mountain hollows are revealed as sparkling jewels in sunlight and black pools under cloud. Often there are sensational glimpses of craggy slopes plunging down into shadowy depths where streams appear as winding silver threads. The narrower the ridge, the greater the enjoyment. Ridgewalking is fellwalking at its best.

There are a few exceptions. For example, the ascent of Scafell by the West Wall Traverse and the fellside crossing to Pillar Rock, each of which leads into situations of unsurpassed grandeur amongst towering crags and give a thrilling sense of adventure without attendant hazards, are not ridge walks but intimate explorations of rock scenery that yield even greater satisfaction to those who seek a measure of excitement in their days on the fells.

Another notable exception is the ascent of Scafell Pike from Borrowdale. This is a classic expedition, and I consider it to be the finest fellwalk in the Lake District. Not because Scafell Pike is the highest ground in the country, not because its summit is especially distinguished, nor even because of the far-reaching panorama it commands, but for the infinite variety of the natural features and landmarks met along the way and the impressive surroundings throughout. It is an ascent of great merit, entailing much rough walking, as befits a climb to this loftiest of all Lakeland fells, and progress is slow, yet every step, if not always a joy to tread, is a step towards the fulfilment of an admirable ambition: to stand on the highest inches in England.

Moreover, there are two routes to the top from Borrowdale, both of rare distinction and abounding in interesting situations, so that the return may be made by using the alternative. By doing so, two splendid fellwalks can be enjoyed in one outing and with a visit to Lakeland's highest cairn as a special incentive, the whole makes a challenging itinerary, a test of endurance for senior citizens and of stamina for youngsters, but well within the capacity of fellwalkers in the average to good bracket; and an achievement that will make the day a day to remember with satisfaction. But there are two buts, the first is to await a spell of settled weather and clear visibility, the other is to start early.

(Opposite) Scafell Pike from Great Gable

Seathwaite, a small farming community

Seathwaite, where the walk starts and ends, is a small farming community, the last outpost in Borrowdale, and the wettest inhabited place in the country in terms of rainfall, averaging about 130 inches a year. Encompassed by steep fells, its river, the Derwent, becomes a raging torrent when in spate and the devastation caused by flood waters is clearly seen in the choke of boulders along its course and in the scattering of debris on the adjoining fields.

Seathwaite is a gateway to the grandest mountains in Lakeland and is a very popular starting point for walks on the fells. The few buildings stand at the terminus of the tarmac road up the valley, and it is not uncommon for dozens of cars to be close-parked on the verge here, while walkers pass through the farmyard from early morning until dusk. Seathwaite is a most friendly place and the farm animals, even the dogs, show no aggression but give the impression that, while everybody is welcome, they are rather bored by the constant procession of visitors. Rainfall statistics notwithstanding, every fellwalker has happy memories of Seathwaite in the morning of a day of adventure and at its close.

From Seathwaite, a path goes forward to Stockley Bridge, a much-trodden pedestrian highway, dusty and scoured of vegetation and seldom without foot traffic. Many visitors to the bridge are ill-shod and not intent on fellwalking expeditions: they settle on the rocks by the stream and after a picnic return to their cars at Seathwaite.

Over the bridge on the facing slope a network of blazed tracks indicate the popular route to Sty Head. This is another example of a well-made path suffering damage by boots descending at speed. The original path, grooved and paved and nicely graded, has been destroyed, only a few small sections remaining in pristine condition.

Stockley Bridge

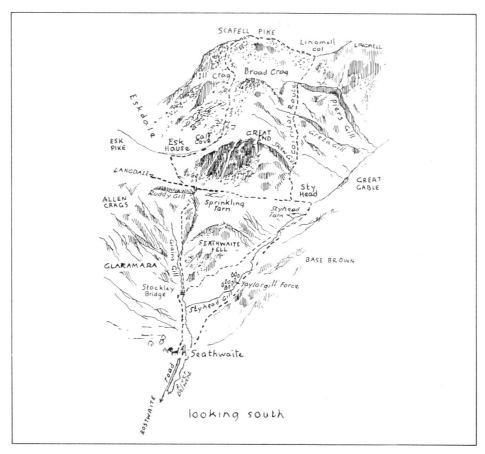

The path to be taken after crossing Stockley Bridge is not the scarred route facing but one turning upstream and entering the narrow confines of Grains Gill, leaving behind the picnic parties and the crowds aiming for Sty Head. Grains Gill is flanked on the left by Glaramara and on the right by Seathwaite Fell; it is quiet and pleasant, with a few trees and water splashes, but near the top, where the stream issues from a ravine, the ground steepens sharply, this being the most arduous part of the walk. Emerging on gentler terrain at the head of the gill, the well-known path linking Great Langdale and Wasdale is reached and, at this point, coming down on the left, is Ruddy Gill, so named because of its red subsoil indicating haematite; this is a continuation of the vein seen exposed at Ore Gap on Bowfell.

Ruddy Gill   *(Above) Grains Gill*

Great End from Sprinkling Tarn

After struggling up and out of Grains Gill, a breather has been earned and this may best be enjoyed by a short stroll to the right along the Wasdale path to Sprinkling Tarn, a most attractive sheet of water with an indented rocky shore, its scenic quality enhanced by the massive cliffs of Great End nearby and soaring above; Great Gable is also in the picture. This is a delightful place, well provided with heathery couches amongst grey boulders on the water's edge. The tarn is an enchantress; the temptation to linger is strong but must be resisted. Too many walkers bound for Scafell Pike have given up the ghost here, daunted by the sight of Great End and bewitched by the beauty and solitude of the tarn.

'Onwards!' must be the cry. Much remains to be done.

(Above) Esk Pike; (opposite) Borrowdale from Great End, with Sprinkling Tarn

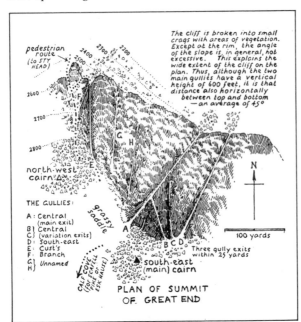

The cliff is broken into small crags with areas of vegetation. Except at the rim, the angle of the slope is, in general, not excessive. This explains the wide extent of the cliff on the plan. Thus, although the two main gullies have a vertical height of 600 feet, it is that distance also horizontally between top and bottom — an average of 45°

pedestrian route (to STY HEAD)

2400
2500
2600
2700
2600
2700
2800

north-west cairn

THE GULLIES:

A: Central (main exit)
B: Central (variation exits)
C: (variation exits)
D: South-east
E: Cust's
F: Branch
G: Unnamed
H:

grassy saddle

CALF COVE (for SCAFELL PIKE or ESK HAUSE)

Three gully exits within 25 yards

south-east (main) cairn

N

100 yards

PLAN OF SUMMIT OF GREAT END

Great End blocks the way to Scafell Pike, but is obviously unassailable by direct assault, and after a reluctant farewell to Sprinkling Tarn the walk is resumed by returning to the head of Grains Gill and following the Langdale path until a cairned track branches off to the right: this is a fairly new short cut to Esk Hause and is a useful time-saver. It rises across a stony slope in the direction of Esk Pike, rounding the cliffs of Great End, and arrives at the grassy saddle of Esk Hause.

At Esk Hause the ground falls away sharply into the wild upper reahes of Eskdale and the great bulk of the Scafells comes in sight, the prominent peak of Ill Crag, a satellite of Scafell Pike and often mistaken for it from this viewpoint, being seen springing from the depths in a succession of crags. Now the path turns to the right and ascends a grassy hollow, Calf Cove, to the skyline above.

Before going on along the path from Calf Cove, an assessment should be made of the strength remaining in the legs and of the hours of daylight still available, because there is an opportunity at this point to make a worthwhile digression to the top of Great End, 2984 ft, at the cost of an extra mile of rough walking up and down the stony slope to the right. On reaching the summit cairn, the justification for this deviation will be fully appreciated: a superb retrospective view of Borrowdale unfolds, extending from Sprinkling Tarn, now seen as an inky blot a thousand feet below, to the fields of the mid-valley and Derwentwater backed by the Skiddaw group. A perambulation along the edge of the cliffs, looking down its impressive gullies, is certainly equally thrilling.

The summit of Great End is rarely visited. It is, in my opinion, a summit much to be preferred to that of Scafell Pike, not only for the Borrowdale view, which is superior to any seen from the Pike but for its quietness and solitude and the excitement and interest of the cliff-top exploration.

At the top of Calf Cove the path to Scafell Pike turns left and is unmistakable, bearing the imprints and footprints and decaying litter of legions of pilgrims and an over-abundance of cairns. At first the going is easy, on grass, but then the ground takes the form of a wide stony ridge with only minor undulations. Next follows 150 yards of close-packed boulders, unavoidable and difficult to negotiate, calling for care. Beyond is an easier section, on gravel and small stones, as the path bypasses the top of Ill Crag, seen on the left and now appearing insignificant, and descends to a col beyond which the path rises as a rough stairway of boulders to skirt the summit of Broad Crag. Stones and outcropping rocks are everywhere in this arid wilderness, cairns marking an uncomfortable passage through them, and patches of mountain greenery are rare indeed. Another small col is reached and ahead now is the final pyramid of Scafell Pike. The path picks a stony way up this last rough slope, steeply initially before easing into a tilted desert of awkward and angular boulders, a dead landscape of sterile rock. Human voices, seeming quite out of place in this lifeless no-man's-land, indicate that the summit is near, and their owners are duly found littering the massive cairn in varying stages of exhaustion and exultation.

The approach to Scafell Pike

The summit of Scafell Pike

Ever since the Ordnance Survey pronounced the height of Scafell Pike as 3210 ft and thereby officially established its superiority in terms of altitude over all other land in the country, its summit has been a magnet for all active visitors to the Lake District, a Mecca that simply must be attained, the objective above all others, the ultimate achievement. Over the years, it has been the venue of ceremonies and celebrations, of bonfires and birthday parties, and the rejoicings continue today with every successful ascent.

Nature's design for the roof of England is a desolation of stones of all shapes and sizes, a barren waste where only mosses and lichens can find sustenance, an inhospitable desert without grace, without charm and without colour other than the drab grey of volcanic rocks.

Man's contribution to the scene is a huge circular stone platform, a plaque commemorating the gift of the summit to the nation; an Ordnance column, and litter. There is no beauty here.

Extract from "The Southern Fells".

Soliloquy.........

In summertime the cairn often becomes over-run with tourists, and a seeker after solitary contemplation may then be recommended to go across to the south peak, where, after enjoying the splendid view of Eskdale, he can observe the visitors to the summit from this distance. He may find himself wondering what impulse had driven these good folk to leave the comforts of the valley and make the weary ascent to this inhospitable place.

Why does a man climb mountains? Why has he forced his tired and sweating body up here when he might instead have been sitting at his ease in a deckchair at the seaside, looking at girls in bikinis, or fast asleep, or sucking ice-cream, according to his fancy. On the face of it the thing doesn't make sense.

Yet more and more people are turning to the hills; they find something in these wild places that can be found nowhere else. It may be solace for some, satisfaction for others : the joy of exercising muscles that modern ways of living have cramped, perhaps; or a balm for jangled nerves in the solitude and silence of the peaks; or escape from the clamour and tumult of everyday existence. It may have something to do with a man's subconscious search for beauty, growing keener as so much in the world grows uglier. It may be a need to re-adjust his sights, to get out of his own narrow groove and climb above it to see wider horizons and truer perspectives. In a few cases, it may even be a curiosity inspired by Wainwright's Pictorial Guides. Or it may be and for most walkers it will be, quite simply, a deep love of the hills, a love that has grown over the years, whatever motive first took them there : a feeling that these hills are friends, tried and trusted friends, always there when needed.

It is a question every man must answer for himself.

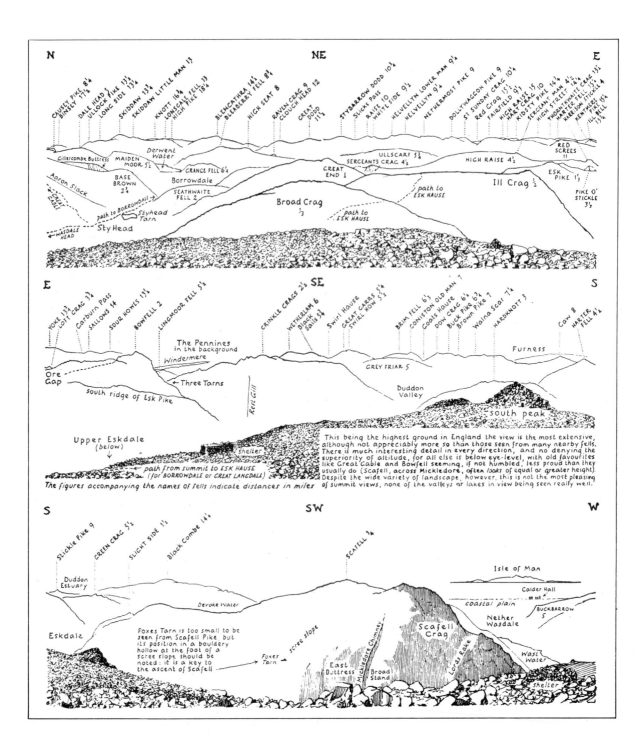

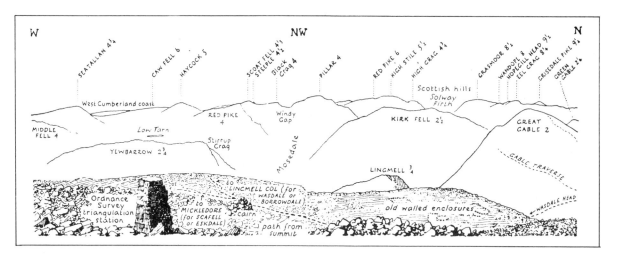

W   NW   N

SEATALLAN 4¼   CAW FELL 6   HAYCOCK 5   SCOAT FELL 4½   STEEPLE 4½   Black Crag 4   PILLAR 4   RED PIKE 6   HIGH STILE 5½   HIGH CRAG 4¼   GRASMOOR 8½   WANDOPE & HOPEGILL HEAD 9½   EEL CRAG 8¼   GRISEDALE PIKE 9½   GREEN GABLE 2¾

West Cumberland coast

Scottish hills
Solway Firth

MIDDLE FELL 4   Low Tarn   RED PIKE 4   Windy Gap   KIRK FELL 2½   GREAT GABLE 2

YEWBARROW 2¼   Stirrup Crag

Mosedale

LINGMELL ¾

GABLE TRAVERSE

Ordnance Survey triangulation station

to LINGMELL COL (for WASDALE or BORROWDALE)

to MICKLEDORE (for SCAFELL or ESKDALE)   cairn

old walled enclosures

WASDALE HEAD

path from summit

Scafell from Scafell Pike

Piers Gill   *Skew Gill*

Rejoicings over, limbs rested, and encouraged by the prospect of easier walking, all mercifully downhill, the return to Seathwaite is started along a distinct but stony path heading west but soon bifurcating, the left branch aiming for Mickledore and Scafell, the right branch, the one to be taken, trending north towards Lingmell and descending to the grassy depression of Lingmell Col. Here a turn to the right, guided by many cairns, soon reaches the head of Piers Gill, an awesome fissure enclosed by vertical cliffs and a notorious trap for inexperienced walkers who enter its lower confines and find themselves stranded in its gloomy depths and unable to proceed, the way being barred by huge chockstones and waterfalls between overhanging crags: an unfortunate adventurer who slipped and fell into the ravine in 1921 was found only after eighteen days of searching by rescue parties, he having survived his injuries and kept himself alive by a trickle of water.

The path skirts the top of the gill and resumes along a grassy shelf with fearful declivities on the left and bouldery slopes on the right. This is the Corridor Route, formerly known as the Guides' Route and originally used by climbers bound for Scafell Crag. It gives a remarkably easy passage through very rough terrain and opens up splendid views of Wasdale Head down on the left and of the tremendous pyramid of Great Gable ahead. The top of another ravine is passed – this is Greta Gill, which drops away sharply on the left and has a magnificent waterfall lower down, unseen from the path – and then follows a steeper descent to the foot of Skew Gill, a huge cleft that splits asunder the stony breast of Great End.

Hopes that there would be no more uphill walking are dashed when the scree debouching from Skew Gill is crossed because the grassy slope beyond must obviously be climbed. This is positively the last ascent of the day, however, and no great obstacle; at the top of the incline the path coming down from Sprinkling Tarn is met as the cliffs of Great End recede, and a turn to the left along this path leads to much-trampled ground very familiar to all who walk on the fells. This is Sty Head Pass, a busy pedestrian thoroughfare and crossroads and a popular springboard for mountain excursions, and the easiest link between Borrowdale and Wasdale. Once it was the subject of fierce controversy when insensitive authorities planned to build a road across it but were howled down by others who had more care and feeling for the environment and were forced to abandon their ridiculous ideas.

Sty Head is for walkers and must remain their exclusive preserve.

Great Gable from the Corridor Route

(Above) Lingmell from Sty Head; (below) Great End from Styhead Tarn

From Sty Head, paths radiate in many directions. To the left as approached (south, turning west), there is a long descent to Wasdale Head, straight ahead begins the climb to the top of Great Gable, and north-east lies Styhead Tarn and the path to Borrowdale, all distinct and profusely cairned. The latter is the one to take. It skirts the western shore of Styhead Tarn, which lacks the scenic attraction of Sprinkling Tarn but is nevertheless a favourite halting place: few walkers go past without stopping for a paddle in its clear waters or for a last look back at the impressive mountain background. This is a wonderful spot, a place of silence and solitude. Fancy wanting to build a motor road through this lonely sanctuary! Motorists must learn to walk if they wish to see the glories of Sty Head.

Taylorgill Force

After leaving Styhead Tarn, Borrowdale-bound, the path runs alongside the issuing stream, Styhead Gill, which becomes the River Derwent down in the valley, and crosses a wooden footbridge to continue the descent to Stockley Bridge. It is infinitely preferable, however, to go forward on the west bank of the stream on a thin track instead of crossing the footbridge. This alternative enters a wooded ravine graced by the slender waterfall of Taylorgill Force, the last highlight of the day. The track precariously hugs the base of a wall of crags, and in a few places needs care, before emerging into marshy fields and slanting down to a bridge by which the Derwent is crossed and Seathwaite entered under an arch in the farm buildings.

Thus ends the best fellwalk of all.

14 SCAFELL
FROM WASDALE HEAD   (6½ MILES)

The mountain landscape of Lakeland is a chaotic upheaval of soaring peaks and lofty ridges springing steeply from deep glacial valleys, a compact mass of high ground rising sharply in wild desolation from a pastoral surround and clearly defined by its geological structure. Much of the upland area is volcanic and the evidences are manifest in a widespread scattering of boulders and stones amongst outcrops where the underlying rock breaks the surface, yet the summits follow no set pattern and are strongly individualistic. There are no smooth grassy hills in the heart of the district: the terrain is rough everywhere, with steep and craggy slopes scoured by scree-filled gullies and choked ravines. Featuring on almost every mountain are precipitous crags, great buttresses of naked rock that both attract and repel, awesome pinnacles fissured by frost and rain. These fearful cliffs are the exclusive preserve of the rock-climber and have no place in the itineraries of the ordinary fellwalker.

The most formidable of these natural bastions is Scafell Crag which towers in supreme majesty above a stony hollow in the fellside: a vertical wall of clean rock some 500 ft high, divided by gullies into five buttresses, the whole appearing to be totally unassailable. 'Nobbut a fleeing thing could get up theer,' said the innkeeper at Wasdale Head when his visitors of a hundred years ago contemplated the possibility of climbing it, yet, despite his assertion, those early pioneers, brave men all, succeeded in devising several routes of extreme severity up those forbidding cliffs, and today there is a network of lines of ascent available only to expert cragsmen.

The aspect of the Crag from below is intimidating, even frightening, and it is so palpably impossible for common or garden mortals to scale that none dares venture up the rocks from the safe ground at the foot, readily acknowledging that those who do so are a superior breed. But Nature has provided a breach in the defences of the Crag by which active walkers may gain access to its innermost secrets, make intimate acquaintance with magnificent and spectacular rock scenery, and emerge unscathed at the top: an achievement earned only by arduous effort and much expenditure of energy. This is the only route on Scafell Crag where walkers can tread safely without encountering serious climbing and without danger to life and limb. Lord's Rake and the West Wall Traverse are special privileges of the fellwalker and make him feel that perhaps he is not too inferior after all.

(Opposite) Scafell from the path to Mickledore from Scafell Pike

(Above) Wasdale Head   *(Right) Pikes Crag and Scafell*

I think Wasdale Head must take pride of place amongst the valleys of Lakeland, not for scenic beauty but because of the sheer grandeur of its mountain setting. It is deeply inurned below steep and shaggy slopes, a patchwork of bright fields intersected by walls of massive width built of stones cleared from the pastures, an emerald strath circumscribed by rough fellsides overtopped by giants: the Scafells, Great Gable and Pillar. There is an inn and a few farmhouses and cottages catering for visitors. Wasdale Head is the best base of all for earnest fellwalkers and climbers.

I remember the inn when it was little changed from the days when that redoubtable dalesman, Will Ritson, was mine host a hundred years ago. On my first visit, it was still a haunt of climbers: boots and ropes cluttered the passages, drying jackets and breeches were draped over doors and chairs, all guests were seated for meals at a large wooden table and given no choice of food, in a room where the furniture showed signs of distress after being subject to demonstrations of climbing techniques; the talk was of climbing and little else, just as in Ritson's time. Ritson was a great character. Rough in speech, spirited in action, a practical joker of ingenuity, he was in no way subservient to the many distinguished men who regularly stayed at the inn and formed the fraternity of rock-climbers, nor was he abashed by their erudite knowledge. It used to be said at that time that Wasdale had the highest mountain, the deepest lake, the smallest church and the biggest liar in England. The biggest liar has gone but his ghost still lives there.

Today, alas, the inn has been brought into line with modern demands. Motorists have discovered Wasdale Head, and sandals are as likely to be seen there as heavy boots. But, seen from the heights around, the valley is as it always was: a place apart, a place unique.

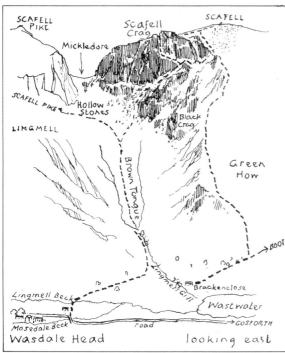

SCAFELL PIKE

Scafell Crag

SCAFELL

Mickledore

SCAFELL PIKE

Hollow Stones

Black Crag

LINGMELL

Brown Tongue

Green How

→ BOOT

Lingmell Gill

Brackenclose

Lingmell Beck

Wastwater

Mosedale Beck

road

→ GOSFORTH

Wasdale Head

looking east

The walk starts at the road corner south of the inn where a signposted path leads to a footbridge crossing Lingmell Beck and then rises along a colourful fellside, the view back to Wasdale Head, with Pillar in the background, being very pleasing as one mounts higher. The path turns left above Lingmell Gill, a stream that bears the scars of devastating cloudbursts, its channel choked by boulders swept down from the heights above by the fury of past floods. But at this point, the attention is rivetted on the exciting skyline that comes into view ahead, formed by the serrated pinnacles of Pikes Crag and, across the Mickledore gap, the shadowed cliffs of the massive upthrust of Scafell Crag.

The gill is crossed at the foot of Brown Tongue, a widening strip of grassland between watercourses, up which climbs a track that would be tedious were it not for the rugged grandeur of the scene ahead, increasing in impressiveness with every step and a spur to progress.

The slope eases at the top of Brown Tongue and the main path inclines left, bound for Scafell Pike. By going forward, a profound hollow is entered amongst a litter of boulders and scree fallen from the enclosing crags. The surroundings are awesome. Pikes Crag soars into the sky on the left, ahead is the gap of Mickledore, topping long fans of scree and rocky debris, and towering on the right the tilted cliffs of Scafell Crag dominate the scene and seem to threaten collapse. This grim fastness is Hollow Stones, and its deep confinement between high and near-vertical walls of rock will make sufferers from claustrophobia and others of timid disposition decidedly uncomfortable. Everybody with a camera will want a picture of Scafell Crag but, seen from below, the aspect is considerably foreshortened, and to view its huge proportions in perspective, a detour along the path rising to Scafell Pike will reveal the full extent of its immense height.

Scafell Crag

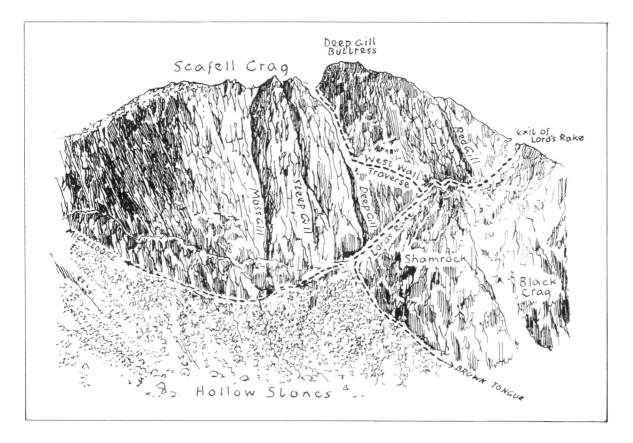

Hollow Stones is the place to gird up the loins before starting the great adventure of ascending to the top of Scafell Crag by the only route available to non-climbing pedestrians, a route of many highlights but accomplished only by sustained and arduous effort. The way goes up the long slope of scree on the right, a toilsome ascent where walkers choose any line they fancy up a ladder of loose and shifting stones, the best footing being found by scrambling upwards along the base of the crags of the Shamrock, so named because from below it appears to be part of the solid mass of Scafell Crag but in fact is severed from it by the deep channel of Lord's Rake, not yet visible. Although the scene around appears to be sterile and dead and unchanged since the landscape took shape in ages past, rockfalls do occur from time to time, caused by frost or heavy rain, and in 1958 a series of violent electrical storms of unusual severity brought down a tremendous tumble of stones and boulders that spread a new covering over the existing scree, and for years after this recent fall could be clearly distinguished by its lighter colour from the drab grey of the older stones.

At the top of the slope any further upward progress seems to be barred by the vertical wall of Scafell Pinnacle directly in front, but at this point a wide channel of stones opens on the right, rising very steeply as straight as a die to a small col on the skyline, and enclosed between a sheer wall of rock on the left and the topmost crags of the Shamrock, the latter forming a high parapet. This is Lord's Rake.

Lord's Rake is unmistakable. It is the only possible way of progressing further upwards from the top of the slope above Hollow Stones, but if confirmation is sought it will be found a few paces to the left, a cross carved in the rock of the Pinnacle marking the spot where four climbers fell to their deaths in 1903, this being still the worst climbing accident in the history of rock-climbing in the district. It should be noted that Lord's Rake does not lead into the heart of the mountain but rises obliquely across the face. Almost at once after entering the confines of the Rake, a huge cleft opens on the left: this is Deep Gill, the most direct route to the summit but seen at a glance to be impossible of ascent by walkers, who are committed to a fierce struggle up the Rake in a chaotic jumble of slippery stones and jammed boulders. Many and varied are the profanities that have been uttered on this desperate treadmill, even by persons of refinement, and all can be forgiven. Despair is lightened occasionally by sightings of starry saxifrage nodding to passers-by from moist crannies in the rocks, but the Rake has no other pleasures. After a strenuous battle against gravity for eighty yards, and just below the col, escape from the Rake is made up a short steep track on the left, where the rock wall relents to permit access to easier ground above. This is the start of the West Wall Traverse.

Lord's Rake

Deep Gill

Deep Gill Buttress and Scafell Pinnacle

After the tortures of Lord's Rake, the West Wall Traverse is sheer delight. Here is grass, at last, on a sloping and rising shelf that doubles back above the lower reaches of the Rake, now out of sight below its confining crags. The rock scenery is spectacular, fascinating, awe-inspiring. The ramparts of Deep Gill Buttress soar into the sky on the right, and directly ahead at close range is the upper part of Scafell Pinnacle, a graceful column of rock tapering to a spire high above. It is a wonderful privilege to be so intimately in the company of such magnificent cliffs. The track on the shelf is rough and boulder-strewn but easy to follow. At the end of the Traverse, it rounds a vertical buttress and enters the upper section of Deep Gill above its difficulties and the top exit is in sight.

The upper section of Deep Gill, a rough channel between impending crags, is tremendously impressive but the climb to the top, although steep, has no problems. It emerges on a level sward on the open fell, a heavenly resting place after all that has been endured. On my first visit, the exit from the gill was defended by an overhanging cornice of vegetation but this final obstacle has been pulled away and the last few yards of ascent, although very steep, are now negotiated by a new track.

The top of the gill, apart from the comfort of its grassy couches, is a wonderfully satisfying place. The view down the gill and across a profound gulf to Great Gable and the fells beyond is of absorbing interest, but the highlight of the scene is Scafell Pinnacle, its topmost rocks now seen in detail nearby on the right, the apex of a sublime pillar of rock that has its roots many hundreds of feet below at the entrance to Lord's Rake.

Scafell Pinnacle from the top of Deep Gill

The summit of Scafell   *Wastwater*

The cairn on the summit of Scafell, 3162 ft, is in view from the top of Deep Gill and is reached in five minutes by a simple stroll across a slight grassy saddle. The top is not particularly distinguished but commands a far-reaching view, being especially good to the south and west where there is a wide prospect of the coast and the sea beyond.

The descent from Scafell, compared with the complexities of the ascent, is simple and straightforward. To avoid the screes falling from the summit, a return is made to the saddle and a stony path going down on the left is followed. To add a spice of interest, a thinner track soon branching to the right and skirting the edge of the crags should be taken in a search for the upper exit of Lord's Rake which is not easy to locate but should be pinpointed and memorised for future expeditions on Scafell: it is a vital link with Hollow Stones and the only pedestrian way off the mountain on its north side, other than the West Wall Traverse, that bypasses Scafell Crag completely and reaches the easier ground below it. The track passes the gaping cleft of Red Gill, down which on my first visit I slithered and tumbled under the wrong impression that it was Lord's Rake, an experience survived without mishap but with pride dented by the mistake. The entrance to the Rake is in fact lower down the slope, around a corner, where its course can be clearly traced, descending to the screes debouching from Red Gill and then rising below cliffs to the col seen earlier in the walk when climbing up the Rake from the other end.

Here end the day's excitements and the walk continues very easily on grass down the long featureless slope of Green How to join the old corpse road linking Wasdale Head and Boot. This is followed down to the right, passing Brackenclose, owned by the Fell and Rock Climbing Club, and going around the head of Wastwater to the valley road, with Wasdale Head a mile distant.

15 GREAT GABLE
FROM HONISTER PASS   (6 MILES)

Great Gable is regarded with affection by all fellwalkers in Lakeland and indeed is probably the peak most favoured for a mountain excursion. The name itself is a challenge and is appropriate, suggesting strength, shapeliness, impressiveness and a commanding presence, and it has all these attributes in full measure. Whenever seen in a view, the distinctive summit is a magnet that draws the feet towards it, appearing from some directions as a slender spire, from others as a dome overtopping the neighbouring fells, and from Wasdale Head, where it was obviously named, it rises sharply from the valley as a massive, steep-sided pyramid that compels the attention of all visitors. The top is an irresistible objective and those who reach it enjoy a sense of achievement. Great Gable has status and confers status on the walkers who attain it.

The mountain is the centre of an area of 3000 acres of high fells acquired by the Fell and Rock Climbing Club as a memorial to the members who lost their lives in the 1914-1918 war, and was given to the National Trust in 1923. In June 1924 a dedicatory tablet, affixed to the summit rocks, was unveiled at a moving ceremony in the presence of a gathering of five hundred fellow-members and friends. Since then, a Remembrance Service has been held here in November each year. The selection of Great Gable as the venue of this annual pilgrimage is testimony to the esteem in which it is held by those who love the hills.

The ascent may be made from several points, the most popular being by the Breast Route from Sty Head, a good way up but too often made noisy by throngs of visitors who do not appreciate that the charm of the mountains lies in their silence and solitude. The direct climb from Wasdale Head is unremittingly steep and threads a stony passage through the fringe of crags high on this flank: it is a weary treadmill and not recommended. The best route, combining a long and interesting walk with the ascent and giving a convenient opportunity to visit other subsidiary summits without digressing, starts from and returns to the top of Honister Pass. I select this route, not because of the advantage gained by taking a car up to the pass which, at 1190 ft, considerably reduces the amount of climbing to be done on foot, but for the scenic excellence of the journey, the easy travelling and the superlative vistas of the Butter- mere valley and fells seen on the way.

(Opposite) Great Gable from Wasdale Head

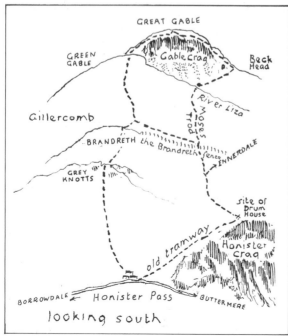

(Left) Honister Crag; (Opposite) The Buttermere Fells

Honister Pass is industrial. Here are the cutting sheds of the immense slate quarries that are slowly carving away and tunnelling into the tall cliffs of Honister Crag, the operation, on a near-vertical plane, being served by an amazing network of steeply inclined roads by which the slate is brought down in great blocks from the quarries high above.

In earlier days, the slate was conveyed down to the sheds by a steep tramway controlled by winding gear in a building near the top known as the Drum House, of which only the foundations remain. It is the track of this old tramway that now provides the way upwards for travellers on foot, and it is a rough and steep start to the walk. Nobody enjoys struggling up and slithering down this straight cut in the fellside but it is a necessary prelude to the expedition and the effort entailed is forgotten when the top is reached and an exciting skyline of fells comes into view. At this point, the more adventurous of walkers may digress to the right to the rim of the quarries and get a startling aerial view of the upper workings from safe stances above. Others, less active, or with no head for exposed heights, should not be tempted from the path which, at the site of the Drum House, turns left across an open moorland.

From the Drum House onwards, the walking is very easy as the path rises gradually along the western flank of Grey Knotts and soon opens up a glorious prospect of Haystacks and the High Stile range, with Pillar beyond and the lake and valley of Buttermere to the right, a picture of great beauty revealing new features as the walk progresses. Although the immediate surroundings are not of great interest, the mile from the Drum House to the Brandreth fence commands charming views to the west, making this easy section of the walk a delightful promenade.

The path from the Drum House had a commercial origin. Before the construction of the gravitation tramways at the Honister quarries, the slate was moved by man-handled sledges down to the Pass, where the road at that time was in a primitive state and not easily negotiable by wheeled traffic, then exclusively horse-drawn. It was more convenient for supplies destined for South Cumberland and the port of Ravenglass to be transported by packhorses across the high fells to Wasdale, the route being planned to avoid steep gradients and rough places. This practice ceased about 1850 when the Honister road was improved, but the path has been kept in being by walkers and is commonly known as Moses' Trod.

Moses is a well-established figure in local tradition, which described him as a Honister quarryman who, after his day's work, illegally made whisky from the bog-water on Fleetwith at his quarry hut, smuggling this potent product to Wasdale with his pony-loads of slate. There is no evidence of his family name, or even that he ever lived, but no reason either for doubting the existence of a man of whom so many legends still survive in the district. He has given his name to many features along the path or in its vicinity. Up amongst the rocks of Gable Crag was a stone hut, now derelict, known as the Smuggler's Retreat, and below it is a rock-climb called Smuggler's Chimney, not climbed by Moses but so named after the first ascent in 1909 out of deference to his memory. On the side of Great Gable overlooking Wasdale, on the route of his descent to that valley, is an upright boulder still known as Moses' Finger.

The path today is most often used as a route of ascent to Great Gable and, after a branch goes away on the right bound for Ennerdale, reaches the Brandreth fence of which only the iron posts remain.

Moses' Finger (8 feet high)

The Brandreth fence

About here, the line of Moses' Trod is obscure, the more distinct path turning left to climb to the ridge between Brandreth and Green Gable en route for Great Gable, but by going forward at the turn on the same contour the Trod becomes clear and can be resumed. I recommend that this should be done: the Trod offers an alternative approach to Great Gable and calls for less effort than the ridge route. Still maintaining a steady contour, the Trod goes towards the great arc of Gable Crag, now starkly in view directly ahead.

Great Gable from Moses' Trod

The Trod crosses a stream, Tongue Beck, hereabouts providing a splendid view of Pillar and the afforested valley of Ennerdale, and then reaches the headwaters of the River Liza in a gloomy and austere setting. The infant river comes down from Stone Cove, a well-named wilderness of boulders between Green Gable, now up on the left, and Gable Crag, which extends in a massive arc high above and directly ahead and forms an impregnable barrier to the summit of Great Gable behind. The terrain is hostile, fans of scree covering the steep slope below the crag. After crossing the stream, Moses' Trod aims diagonally to the right and crosses the depression of Beck Head thence descending to Wasdale, but this is an unnecessary digression when the target is the top of Great Gable, and a slanting route upwards, heading for the skyline to the right of Gable Crag, leads to the stony ridge coming up from Beck Head, and here a steep and stony track goes up to the left and emerges on the tilted plateau of the summit, the highest point being clearly in view and reached along a track indicated by many cairns.

The summit of Great Gable; (right) The war memorial tablet

The summit of Great Gable is an upthrust of bare rock surmounted by a large cairn, a hallowed place since its adoption as a war memorial; the dedicatory tablet, which has a relief map of the area carved on it, is affixed to a rock on the north side. I have a personal interest in this summit: it was here that a Southport fellwalker spent a day in 1966 collecting signatures on a petition recommending me for a national honour following the completion of my series of Lakeland guidebooks, this being duly awarded. I was not to know the identity of this friendly and appreciative walker until fourteen years later when it was disclosed to me by a correspondent who knows him.

As may be expected from the superior altitude of the summit, 2949 ft, the view from it is excellent in all directions.

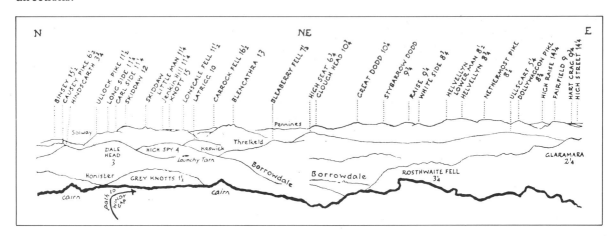

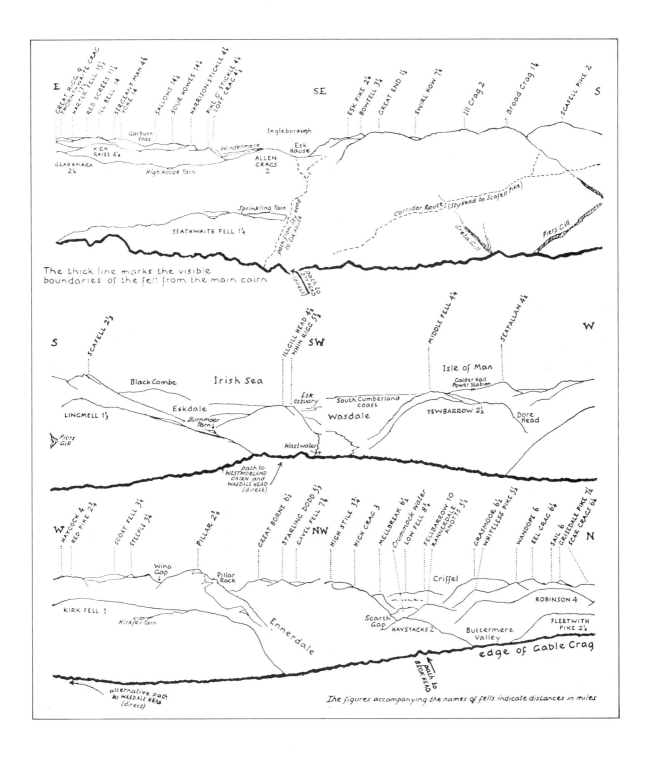

The thick line marks the visible boundaries of the fell from the main cairn

The figures accompanying the names of fells indicate distances in miles

(Opposite) Wasdale from Great Gable with Wastwater in the distance; (right) View past Windy Gap; (below) Gable Crag from Green Gable

The summit plateau should not be left without first taking a short stroll of 120 yards south-west in the direction of Wasdale to a prominent cairn (the Westmorland Cairn) standing on the edge of a downfall of crags and having an arresting view of Wasdale Head, a patchwork of small fields half a mile below, and of Wastwater in the distance beyond. There is also to be seen from this point the massive build-up of the Scafells from valley level to the sky-line ridge, with the great gash of Piers Gill prominent. Nearby, below the cairn, the upper rocks of the Napes appear as a serrated fringe in front of a profound void.

All paths on the top of Great Gable are abundantly cairned. The way off for the return journey to Honister heads north at first but is deflected east by the brink of Gable Crag, dropping steeply amid rocks to join a path slanting to the neat col of Windy Gap. Stone Cove is now down on the left and descending on the right is the ravine of Aaron Slack, carrying a track to Sty Head. Across the gap, there is a short climb to the top of Green Gable, 2603 ft. The summit is pleasant, with unseen cliffs falling from the west edge. The dominant feature in the scene from this viewpoint is Gable Crag, its full height and impressiveness clearly revealed at close range.

From the top of Green Gable, the way onwards is clear, continuing along the spine of a ridge that forms a watershed between the gathering grounds of the rivers Liza and Cocker to the west and those of the Derwent to the east. There is now, for the first time on the walk, an outlook over the deep trench of Borrowdale beyond the hanging valley of Gillercomb, steeply buttressed and carrying Sourmilk Gill down to Seathwaite around the abrupt height of Base Brown. A path branches off in this direction, but the way goes forward, still aiming north, and descends to a depression beyond which rises the slope of Brandreth. At this depression, the path inclines left and descends to join Moses' Trod at the Brandreth fence, from where the route of the outward journey can be reversed to the Drum House and Honister Pass, but a better alternative that avoids any retracing of steps is to go up to the summit of Brandreth, 2344 ft.

The top of Brandreth is stony and featureless, having nothing of nearby interest, and only the extensive panorama is likely to delay progress. The summit cairn is sited at a meeting of three broken fences, the one heading north-east pointing to the next objective, Grey Knotts, reached by a simple walk along a wide ridge.

The summit of Brandreth, looking to Great Gable

(Above) Tarn on the summit of Grey Knotts;
(right) Honister Pass from Grey Knotts

The summit of Grey Knotts, 2287 ft, is, in contrast to that of Brandreth, quite attractive, having a series of tors of grey rock and a few small tarns, the habitat of bog bean. This is a lovely place for the last rest of the day and a final appraisal of the beautiful views in all directions; this too is the place to wave farewell to Great Gable. In mist, the summit can be confusing and it is important not to drift eastwards where there are crags. In clear conditions there is no difficulty, the north edge revealing a view of Honister Pass and the cutting sheds and the parked cars a thousand feet below. There is no distinct path down but no hazards arise from making a beeline over rough and bumpy ground to the luxury of the tarmac road.

16 THE MOSEDALE HORSESHOE
FROM WASDALE HEAD   (8 MILES)

YEWBARROW   Dore Head   RED PIKE   SCOAT FELL   STEEPLE   Black Crag   Wind Gap   PILLAR   Pillar Rock

Bull Crags   Blackem Head   High Level Traverse   Looking Stead   Black Sail Pass

Mosedale Beck   Mosedale   Gatherstone Beck   KIRK FELL

Ritson's Force

GOSFORTH   road   Wasdale Head   looking north west

There are five Mosedales in the Lake District, the name signifying a dreary and desolate valley, often marshy, and the choice is appropriate for most of them. But not for the best known, the Mosedale that lies in a deep recess opening from the head of Wasdale but out of the sight of visitors to that valley. Desolate and wild it certainly is, but no lover of mountain scenery would ever consider it dreary. The dale is encompassed by lofty fells of extreme roughness and grandeur, the highest being Pillar, one of Lakeland's giants, but it is not Pillar that catches the eye when Mosedale is surveyed from its entrance but the shadowed front of Red Pike, a cataract of beetling crags of intimidating appearance, and to a lesser degree the steep slopes of Scoat Fell beyond. Except for a stony track coming down from a col at the head, the valley has no paths other than those made by sheep, nor is likely to have, the terrain being too uninviting to attract sightseers although an exciting place for adventurers and explorers.

Mosedale is terminated abruptly at Blackem (or Black Comb) Head, an untrodden wilderness, a tangle of crags and rocky gorges and hidden waterfalls where the starry saxifrage lives happily without disturbance. But above, along the skyline, is a path that makes a high-level circuit of the tops around the valley, an exhilarating expedition with no obstacles to easy progress. This splendid walk can be, and should be, augmented by two worthwhile detours from the ridge path, one to the wonderful and famous Pillar Rock, cathedral-like and majestic, and the other to the lovely summit of Steeple. The walk to be described will include these detours.

(Opposite) Pillar from High Stile

Mosedale from the path to Gatherstone Beck

It is preferable to do the round of Mosedale anti-clockwise for two reasons: first, to avoid the steep initial climb to Dore Head which is too overfacing after a hearty breakfast and, secondly, to approach Pillar Rock from the best direction for seeing it to full advantage.

The walk starts along the lane beyond the inn at Wasdale Head and reaches open ground at the foot of Kirk Fell, where a good path turns to the left above the tree-lined course of Mosedale Beck. This contours the slope before gradually inclining upwards to Gatherstone Beck.

On one occasion I was coming down this path when I came across four elderly walkers, two men and their wives, who were halted in some distress; in fact, one of the women was lying on the ground. She had broken an ankle, they told me: what could they do? I offered to report the accident at Wasdale Head, which I did, and was asked to accompany two local volunteers and help to carry a stretcher. I agreed with some reluctance, having already had a tiring walk that day, and off we went. The stretcher had an iron frame and was heavy. It was heavier still when the casualty was loaded on it but we managed to bring her down to the inn where, to my amazement, she limped across the yard to the party's car and they drove away without a word of thanks. Obviously she had not broken an ankle but merely suffered a sprain and could very well have been supported down by her companions. I am sure that incidents of this sort happen often, the rescue teams being called out unnecessarily. Too many people these days seem to regard voluntary help, not only on the hills, as a social service to which they are entitled as members of the Welfare State; they have lost the inclination to fend for themselves. While the rescue teams prefer to do their Good Samaritan work without pay, I feel strongly that those who need their help, or think they do, should make a generous donation to the funds of these brave and unselfish men.

The path rises steadily and crosses Gatherstone Beck, a very attractive watercourse enlivened by sparkling cascades along a bouldery channel, and continues to climb on the opposite slope, swinging right above zigzags to reach Black Sail Pass where a turn to the left alongside an old fence leads up to the grassy plateau of Looking Stead. Or, above the zigzags, advantage can be taken of a short cut branching left and climbing more directly to the skyline at Looking Stead. Now the east ridge of Pillar is clearly seen and there is a view down into Ennerdale, a dark shroud of coniferous forest. I remember the time when this valley was bare of trees and was colourful and pleasant. Its former beauty has gone.

(Left) Gatherstone Beck; (below) Ennerdale from Looking Stead

The ridge is now followed and if persisted in will duly reach the summit of Pillar, but a watch should be kept for a track going down the fellside on the right at the foot of a steep rise in the ridge. This track avoids a small crag directly ahead by rounding it below and rising again beyond. Originally, before this track was devised, it was usual to cross the face of the crag, rather precariously, by shuffling along a horizontal crack.

This is the start of the High Level Traverse to Pillar Rock and the start of one of the best miles in Lakeland, a route of engrossing interest. With little variation in contour, it proceeds along an easy shelf below an array of formidable crags high on the left, the fellside on the right dropping steeply into Ennerdale. The track is delightful and steps are accelerated by the exciting prospect of an early sighting of Pillar Rock, as yet sensed rather than seen. The crowning moment arrives at the top of a small rise where stands Robinson's Cairn, the soaring cliffs of Pillar Rock here being fully revealed ahead: a wonderful sight, spectacular and awe-inspiring.

The cairn is a memorial to John Wilson Robinson, a pioneer fellwalker and rock-climber, a man sincerely devoted to the fells, an enthusiast of great energy who regularly walked from his home at Lorton to join his friends at Wasdale Head for a day's climbing and then walked back home in the evening: a prodigious performance involving some twenty miles of rough up and down tramping apart from the day's activities at Wasdale Head. A memorial tablet, beautifully worded, is affixed to a nearby rock.

The High Level Traverse

Pillar Rock from Robinson's Cairn

Wordsworth wrote of Pillar:

> You see yon precipice; it almost looks
> Like some vast building made of many crags;
> And in the midst is one particular rock
> That rises like a column from the vale,
> Whence by our shepherds it is called the Pillar.

The foot of Pillar Rock can be reached from Robinson's Cairn by a simple crossing on grass amongst outcrops but would lead into a trap from which no escape was possible. This is definitely not the way to go. Instead the track, which now turns left and ascends into a cove, should be adhered to closely and followed along an easy terrace rising to the right above a tremendous downfall of rock. This is the Shamrock Traverse, so named because the crag immediately below, which is severed from Pillar Rock by the deep cleft of Walker's Gully, appears from the east to be part of the main mass.

Excitement becomes intense as the Shamrock Traverse rises to confront the upper part of Pillar Rock, the High Man, and reveals its intimate detail at close range. The scene is overpowering. Thoughts are of nothing else but the immense tower of rock immediately ahead. Worldly worries are totally excluded from the mind, and even toothache can be forgotten in such sensational surroundings. The scene is sublime, yet brutal, without a shred of beauty, and indeed to timid observers will seem a place of horror, awful and ugly.

The Shamrock Traverse

High Man, Pillar Rock

There is no cause for concern if the sketchy track is kept underfoot as it mounts through a tangle of boulders to crag-free but stony ground above the Rock which, on looking back, now appears as a huge dome partly screened by an intervening height. The track continues steeply upwards.

I was once toiling up this slope and nearing the top when I was hailed by a party of men far below on the fellside, and it was obvious from their gesticulations that this was no ordinary greeting, but the distance was too great for their shouts to be intelligible. I went on, rather mystified, and was to learn later that the men were searching for a walker who had set out for Pillar the previous day and not returned. They must have thought that I may have been the missing person, but they continued their search and found the man lying dead at the foot of Walker's Gully.

Gradually the gradient eases and the track emerges on the grassy plateau of Pillar's summit, the Rock being lost to sight and, after the intricacies of the ascent, the open landscape is a welcome change.

The top of Pillar is the only smooth place on this rugged mountain and, except for a summit cairn at 2927 ft and a triangulation column, has little of interest. The view, however, is excellent, the full length of the Scafell range and Great Gable being particularly well seen.

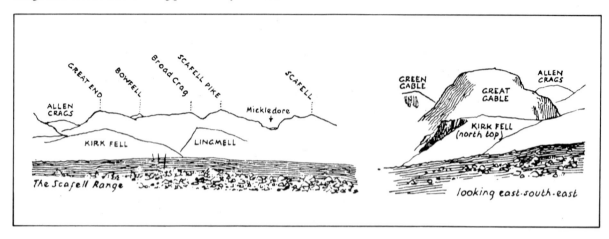

One of my evergreen memories is of a February day fifty years ago when I first visited Pillar. I climbed straight up from Ennerdale, which at that time had not been planted with conifers and was bare and desolate. I had not gone far when I was enveloped in a clammy mist, visibility being reduced to a few yards only. I had hoped to see Pillar Rock, having been thrilled by graphic reports of rock-climbing adventures on this wonderful monolith, but the blanket of mist blotted out everything except a few yards of ground around me. This flank of Pillar is one of the roughest in the district, a succession of craggy outcrops, and upward progress was laborious. Robbed of sight I struggled ever upwards, mercifully without meeting any insuperable obstacle. The mist did not relent, even for a moment, and the silence was profound: this was not a day for larks to be flying and singing. I did not bump into Pillar Rock and saw no sign of it. I began to sense that I was well off-course, this being confirmed when at long last I entered a scree gully that led me to the skyline of the west ridge some distance from the summit. I had spent four hours struggling up the rugged fellside like a blind man, seeing nothing beyond my grasp. I do not recall a mist as dense and immovable as this . . .

The incident would not be worth the telling but for a remarkable transformation that occurred as I walked up to the summit. All at once, with a suddenness that transfixed me, I stepped out of the wet mist into brilliant and dazzling sunlight and above was a cloudless blue sky. I went up to the summit, now starkly clear. It was a walk in space. Just below me was the mist, stretching into the far distance but now having a ceiling and being no longer grey but a pure white. Clearly defined on this vaporous curtain was the shadow of a man. It was my shadow, walking when I walked, stopping when I stopped: the first time I had witnessed such a phenomenon. I spent a few minutes waving to the man in the mist, always getting a simultaneous response and then, as I went on down the east ridge, there was a gradual movement in the mist, then a swirling and boiling of the vapours followed by a swift dispersal and disappearance. In a matter of minutes, the mist vanished to disclose the valley below and the fells beyond. The rest of the day, as I went down to Wasdale Head and over to Eskdale, was gloriously sunny and warm.

Windgap Cove

The remainder of the route around the Mosedale skyline can be prospected from the top of Pillar and promises straightforward walking. First comes a rough descent south-west to the narrow col of Wind Gap, neatly dividing Mosedale and Ennerdale and carrying a path between the two valleys, the Ennerdale side being a scene of wild desolation with a ring of crags surrounding the lonely hollow of Windgap Cove.

Across the col, there is a sharp rise to the top of Black Crag, the path then levelling to give easy progress on grass above the crag, which falls precipitously into Windgap Cove. From the edge of the cliffs, a striking view is obtained of the slender pinnacle of Steeple, here seen springing high out of gloomy depths, its lofty and delicate proportions justifying its name. The gulf between, bounded by the crags of Scoat Fell, is the grim recess of Mirk Cove, an area of devastation uninviting and repelling.

After leaving Black Crag, the next objective is the summit of Scoat Fell, 2760 ft, reached by an easy uphill trudge made more interesting by keeping to the edge overlooking Mirk Cove. The naming of mountain hollows as coves is uncommon in Lakeland, occurring only along this Ennerdale flank and in the Helvellyn range. On the top of Scoat Fell, a track goes down to Steeple, now below eye level, and reaches its summit by a short scramble. This is a detour strongly recommended. The summit, 2687 ft, is only a few yards in extent and poised above a tremendous precipice; it is a delectable spot for a halt and an appraisal of the impressive scenes around. Here one is a king on a throne.

Returning to the broad top of Scoat Fell, the turning point of the journey, the route heads southeast down a long slope skirting the head of Mosedale to a depression followed by a sharp climb to the summit of Red Pike, 2707 ft, along the edge of cliffs that plunge steeply down into Mosedale.

(Right) Steeple from Black Crag

The Chair

Red Pike's summit cairn is a fine viewpoint, enhanced by its dramatic situation on the brink of crags, Great Gable and the Scafell range in particular forming an imposing background, but there is little else of interest. Further along the declining ridge is another major cairn and nearby, 20 yards from the path, is a feature not often noticed: a rocky outcrop provides a seat to which has been added a backrest and arms of stones. This is The Chair, a well-known and popular objective of walkers a century ago who spoke of climbing to The Chair as the visitors of today speak of climbing Red Pike. Still in pristine condition, The Chair has withstood all storms but is not proof against vandalism and should be respected.

Now every step of the way back is downhill, which is not to say that all is plain sailing from here onwards, for Dore Head, shunned earlier in the day, has still to be faced. This depression, quickly reached from Red Pike, occurs below the steep rocky slope of Yewbarrow beyond and from it there descends into Mosedale a long strip of bare ground that formerly had a deep covering of small stones and was the best and fastest scree-run in the district: an experienced walker, simply by digging his heels in the scree, could be carried down by the moving stones in a few minutes. Now all has changed. Most of the stones have been scraped away by over-use, leaving the strip as an ugly scar, slippery and dangerous for anyone descending at speed. It is advisable to come down the grass verges although this practice must inevitably result in a widening of the scar.

Ritson's Force

At the foot of this scree-run, a track swings to the right and comes down alongside Mosedale Beck, here fringed by trees and having a pleasant feature in the small waterfall of Ritson's Force. Then the walk ends happily with a stroll through fields and a crossing of the old packhorse bridge at Wasdale Head.

Packhorse bridge, Wasdale Head

The High Stile range, forming a mountainous barrier between the parallel valleys of Ennerdale and Buttermere, is one of the most beautiful of ridge walks. It is, moreover, free from complexities, rising on a straight north-west – south-east axis without deviations. Three summits overtop the general level of the ridge, High Stile being the central and highest, and High Crag and Red Pike, little lower in altitude, being sturdy supporters on each side. Both flanks are steeply scarped, High Stile and High Crag having precipitous crags on the Buttermere side, and there are conifer plantings along their bases although not extending high enough above Buttermere to mar the impressive grandeur of the scene. Red Pike is gentler and has a scattering of deciduous trees on its lower slopes. The range makes a tremendous background to the Buttermere valley and lake, this being the finest aspect, a picture of surpassing beauty even by Lakeland standards. Approaches from Ennerdale are much less attractive, the afforested area being much more extensive and developed without regard to the environment, and the slopes above too steep and rough to be considered; a path climbs to Red Pike from a break in the plantations but lacks interest and scenic quality. It is the ascent from Buttermere that reveals the grandest features of the range and excels in loveliness and charm: every step is a delight.

Duplication of place names occurs in many instances in Lakeland, often causing confusion. This Red Pike is commonly referred to as the Buttermere Red Pike to distinguish it from the one overlooking Mosedale.

It is usual to reach the ridge by using a well-worn path climbing above the village of Buttermere to the summit of Red Pike, thereafter following the ridge over High Stile and High Crag and descending the screes of Gamlin End to Scarth Gap. The path up to Red Pike is very popular, having a midway attraction in Bleaberry Tarn, but tends to be over-populated by visitors on summer days. There appears to be no other line of ascent to the ridge, but there is, just one, and this I recommend to active walkers who prefer solitude and do not mind a rough scramble. This is certainly the way for me.

I found this route when once scouting in Burtness Comb for a way to the top of High Crag as an alternative to the customary line of ascent from Scarth Gap up the unpleasant and slippery screes of Gamlin End. I noticed what appeared to be a continuous shelf rising steeply across the face of High Crag's tremendous north buttress, a thousand feet high, and on exploring further had no difficulty in following it upwards to broken ground just below the north top, the summit then being a short distance forward. I was pleased with this discovery for several reasons: it seemed to be a virgin route, having no traces of earlier visitors; it gave a feeling of adventure and real mountaineering; it led directly to the top of the mountain; it was profoundly quiet, there being nobody within sight or sound, and never again did I need to toil up or down Gamlin End. This is the route I shall describe.

(Opposite) High Stile from Gatesgarth

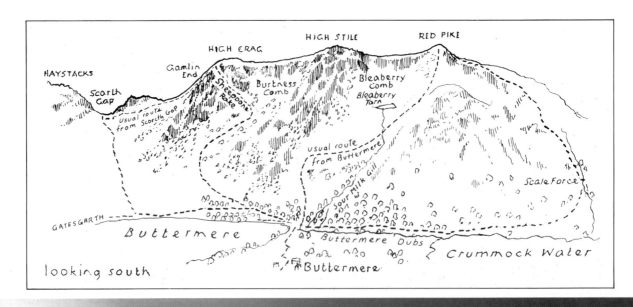

From Buttermere village, a lane leads to a bridge crossing the stream issuing from the lake and beyond is a choice of paths, the one to be taken turning left through the lakeside wood. This is departed from 120 yards beyond a cross-wall where a forest ride branches to the right, soon reaching a stile in another wall, over which a track travels in company with it, rising to the wide opening of Burtness Comb, also known as Birkness Comb. This track has been fashioned by rock-climbers bound for the crags around the Comb, a favourite area for their sport. When the wall turns away left, a line of cairns indicates the way forward to the inner recesses of the Comb and discloses the ring of cliffs ahead. On the left is the tremendous precipice of High Crag, and rising across it will be noticed a shelf or gangway that offers a tenuous line of escape to the skyline high above. This is the way to go: it deserves a name and I call it Sheepbone Rake, which is appropriate because the only officially named feature hereabouts is Sheepbone Buttress, a crag alongside. A rough slope is climbed to the foot of the Rake and the route continues steeply up it as a scramble on grass with no impediments other than fallen boulders and no insuperable obstacles. The situation, poised between crags above and crags below, is sensational but safe. At the top, broken ground is encountered and a climb to the right reaches the north cairn of High Crag and the summit a short walk beyond.

(Opposite) Buttermere   *(Below) High Crag from Burtness Comb*

The summit cairn of High Crag, decorated with discarded iron fence posts, stands at 2443 ft on the extreme eastern edge of the ridge and commands uninterrupted views in that direction, the finest aspect being of the head of Ennerdale backed by Great Gable and Kirk Fell, the latter overtopped by the Scafell group. Nearer and below eye level are Scarth Gap and Haystacks, with Fleetwith Pike a bold object to their left, the extensive panorama culminating in the distant skyline of the Helvellyn range.

The head of Ennerdale

Burtness Comb

With the hard work of the day over, the exhilarating ridge walk to follow can be contemplated with anticipatory pleasure. It is a joy to tread, not only for its intrinsic delights but also for the beautiful views it provides as the walk proceeds. There is a short descent from High Crag and the path then skirts the edge of the crags falling into Burtness Comb, the most arresting feature being the vertical face of Eagle Crag, one of the many so-named in the district, confirming that these magnificent birds were once permanent residents. There are spectacular glimpses down into the depths of the Comb along this edge. Lakeland really needs a uniform name for its mountain hollows: the Welsh have 'cwm', the Scots 'corrie', but here they are variously named as 'comb', 'combe', 'cove' and even 'hole'. Burtness Comb is one of the most typical of these hollows forming a hanging valley, wild and lonely, above the cultivated pastures of the lowland farms.

When the Comb is passed, a simple but stony path rises gradually to the highest point on the ridge, the summit of High Stile, 2644 ft, presenting a view that evokes raptures of delight from its cairn perched on the brink of an abrupt drop and justifying an hour's rest to absorb the beauty of the scene.

(Opposite) Crummock Water; (above) Fleetwith Pike from High Stile; (below) Red Pike from High Stile

The cairn on High Stile is left, always with reluctance, and the walk resumed, a short descent leading to the obvious continuation of the ridge towards Red Pike. There are impressive peeps down the gullies of Chapel Crags as the path rounds another comb, a twin to Burtness but less rocky. This is Bleaberry Comb, identified by the dark pool of Bleaberry Tarn on the floor of another hanging valley, and across it can be seen the usual route to Red Pike coming up from Buttermere. The ridge path prefers the open fell top, but more interest will be found by skirting the edge of the escarpment and smug satisfaction derived from the sight of walkers toiling up the scree of the tourist route below. Then, after a slight ascent, the summit of Red Pike, 2479 ft, is reached.

It will have been noticed on the walk from High Crag that all the excitement and beauty of the ridge is concentrated on the Buttermere side, the Ennerdale flank contributing nothing, but hereabouts Pillar is an imposing object across the latter valley.

A direct return may be made to Buttermere from the summit of Red Pike by using the tourist path, but the ridge is not yet ended although declining steadily from here onwards. By continuing in the same direction, another comb is brought into view, also having a rim of crags descending into a hanging valley and generally following the pattern of the others. This is Ling Comb, a place of heather, but unfrequented, a Cinderella that nobody comes to see. The rim of the escarpment is known as Lingcomb Edge. It is followed down to its extremity, where a heathery slope is descended to the watercourse of Scale Beck, seen forming a defined channel on the left. A path materialises alongside the stream, becoming steep in its lower stages and eroded by visitors to the lovely waterfall now just below.

High Stile from Red Pike

Scale Force

On a walk of many highlights, here is another. The waterfall is Scale Force, the highest in the district and one of the finest. It plunges in a single leap of over 100 feet down a dark ravine hemmed in by perpendicular walls bedecked by ferns and trees: a wonderful sight.

A beaten path descends from the outlet of the ravine towards Crummock Water, which, in Victorian times, had a boat-landing to which ladies and gentlemen were rowed across the lake from Buttermere as part of a popular excursion to the waterfall. This facility has long been defunct and so have the ladies and gentlemen, at least in sartorial appearance. Most of today's visitors are rough shod and not at all elegant, and for them there is no alternative to the lakeside path that continues pleasantly amongst trees to the bridge at Buttermere but is notoriously wet underfoot. Still, wet feet don't matter at the end of a perfect day.

18 HAYSTACKS
FROM BUTTERMERE   (7 MILES)

Dear Haystacks! Here is a rugged height, little in stature and small in extent, encircled by much loftier fells, some of international renown, yet standing quite unabashed by their greater presence in the landscape and not acknowledging inferiority to any of them. Like a shaggy and undisciplined terrier in the midst of a company of sleek foxhounds, Haystacks looks irascible, defiantly aggressive, and a bad-tempered little monster, not caring a damn for anybody or anything, and if blessed with lungs would probably demand attention by yapping and barking all day long. It is unusual in structure, not conforming to any pattern and stoutly asserting its right to be called a mountain despite a lack of height, a superior mountain because it is certainly not prepared to concede that any of its neighbours, not even Great Gable and Pillar, which look down at it, are more imposing or important. It probably feels infuriated by appearing last in this book, knowing jolly well that its rightful place is first.

So why does Haystacks win the affection of all walkers? You have to climb to the top and wander about to understand. Above the wall of defending crags is a fascinating landscape, a confusing labyrinth of miniature peaks and tors, of serpentine tracks in rampant heather, of lovely tarns and tarnlets, of crags and screes, of marshes and streams, of rocks for climbing and rocks not for climbing, of surprises around every corner, with magnificent views all around. Adrenalin runs fast in this natural wonderland. For a man trying to forget a persistent worry, the top of Haystacks is a complete cure.

Haystacks is absolutely right in demanding special attention, although perhaps exaggerating in claiming a degree of superiority over all other fells in the district. To say that there are few to match it would be a fairer assessment of relative merits.

The approach should always be made from Buttermere village to introduce into the walk the sylvan beauty of trees and water as an appetising starter and to emphasise the contrasting wildness soon to follow. A shorter version is possible from a car parked near Gatesgarth at the head of the lake, but Haystacks deserves better than to be cut short and needs the gradual appreciation that the longer route gives. Buttermere's lake is too regular in outline to rank with the best, but its rocky shoreline, fringed by trees, is quite delightful and served by an enchanting path that has Haystacks in view all the way.

(Opposite) Haystacks from the north shore of Buttermere

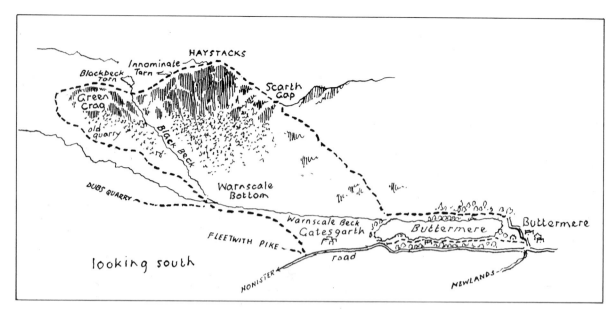

The lakeside path leaves the village at once and keeps closely to the north shore, at one point passing through a tunnel cut in the rocks, and is everywhere charming. Near the head of the lake, the path joins the Honister motor road and this is then followed past the large farm of Gatesgarth, the last outpost in the valley and, like Seathwaite in Borrowdale, well known to all walkers, to the point where an intake wall goes off to the right at the foot of Fleetwith Pike. The white cross now prominently in view on the lower slopes of the Pike was erected as a memorial to Fanny Mercer, killed in a fall on the nearby rocks in 1887. Here the road is left and a path taken alongside the wall to enter the gloomy amphitheatre of Warnscale Bottom, the cliffs of Haystacks being directly ahead and high above.

Haystacks and High Crag

A direct assault on Haystacks from Warnscale Bottom is seen at a glance to be totally out of the question, and a rising detour must be made to avoid and get above its daunting crags. Had it not been for an old Ordnance map, I would probably never have been aware of a disused track that climbs across the fellside to an abandoned quarry below Green Crag. One day I set out to try to trace it, and found it to be still distinct in places with ancient cairns still surviving to mark its many zigs and zags: a fascinating stairway. To get a footing on this track, it is necessary to cross Warnscale Beck, which is easier said than done, near its confluence with Black Beck. Upon reaching the quarry and the end of the track, the slope beyond is climbed to the ridge where a turn to the right, again on a good path, skirts the summit of Green Crag and brings into view an exciting prospect ahead. Blackbeck Tarn is seen occupying a lonely hollow on the left, its issuing stream falling away sharply into a ravine, and the path winding sinuously forward, crossing the outflow and rising along the base of crags to the top of Haystacks, now seen cut away abruptly by precipitous cliffs.

Haystacks from Green Crag

(Above) Blackbeck Tarn; (below) Innominate Tarn looking towards Great Gable

After fording Black Beck and looking fearfully down its steep channel, the path hugs the base of a wall of rock and, when clear of this, a choice of routes is available. By wandering to the left over a rough carpet of heather and mosses the Brandreth fence will be met and the walk can be extended by inclining to the right and climbing through a maze of outcrops to the summit. Or, by scrambling up the broken slope to the right, the rim of the crags plunging down to Warnscale Bottom comes suddenly underfoot with dramatic effect, the edge then being followed upwards above a sensational downfall of steep gullies and steeper buttresses, having throughout in stark contrast the gentle beauty of Buttermere as a backcloth, until the summit is reached. Or the main path may be continued, aiming more directly for the highest point of the fell and passing the lovely Innominate Tarn, a delectable spot.

perched boulder on a rock platform

typical summit tors

the summit

The summit cairn stands on a rocky tor amid a confusion of boulders, its modest elevation of 1900 ft seeming to be incongruously low, for surely this is the top of an Alpine giant? The views are magnificent, Great Gable and Pillar and High Crag all being prominent in a glorious panorama. No wonder that Haystacks has such a good opinion of itself.

Buttermere from Haystacks

Scarth Gap

The temptation to linger on the top of Haystacks until the sun goes down must be resisted for the descent to Scarth Gap, passing a charming rocky tarnlet, is rough and getting rougher as more walkers become addicted to Haystacks, sliding screes having to be negotiated before easy ground is reached at the gap. But, having survived this ordeal, the way back to Buttermere is simple, a good path descending grassy slopes to the head of the lake, whence a much-trodden track goes alongside the shore, entering a plantation and continuing distinctly through trees to the bridge over the stream issuing from the lake, where a lane leads to the village. What a day it has been!

(Opposite) High Crag from Haystacks   *(Below) Buttermere*